MODERN CATALAN POETRY:
AN ANTHOLOGY

Poems selected and translated
from the Catalan by:
David H. Rosenthal

MODERN CATALAN POETRY: AN ANTHOLOGY

Poems selected and translated
from the Catalan by:
David H. Rosenthal

New Rivers Press 1979

Poems in this volume have appeared in the magazines *Centerpoint*, *Greenhouse*, *The Humanist* and *Invisible City*, in *New Directions 31*, and in Mr. Rosenthal's own book of poems *Eyes on the Street* (New York: Barlenmir House, 1974). Portions of the introduction were originally published in *The Nation*. Thanks and acknowledgement are due the poets and their publishers for permission to reprint and translate their works, and to Galería Trece, Galeria René Metràs and Galeria Maeght in Barcelona, Galería Vandré's in Madrid, Nathan Silverberg and Edicions Polígrafa for the use of the artwork.

This book has been published with the aid of grants from the National Endowment for the Arts and the New York State Council on the Arts.

This book was manufactured in the United States of America for New Rivers Press (C.W. Truesdale, editor/publisher) 1602 Selby Avenue, St. Paul, Minnesota 55104 in a first edition of 2000 copies.

**FOR MY THREE FRIENDS IN THIS BOOK:
FRANCESC PARCERISAS, MARTA PESSARRODONA, and
RAMON PINYOL**

MODERN CATALAN POETRY

CATALAN ARTWORK

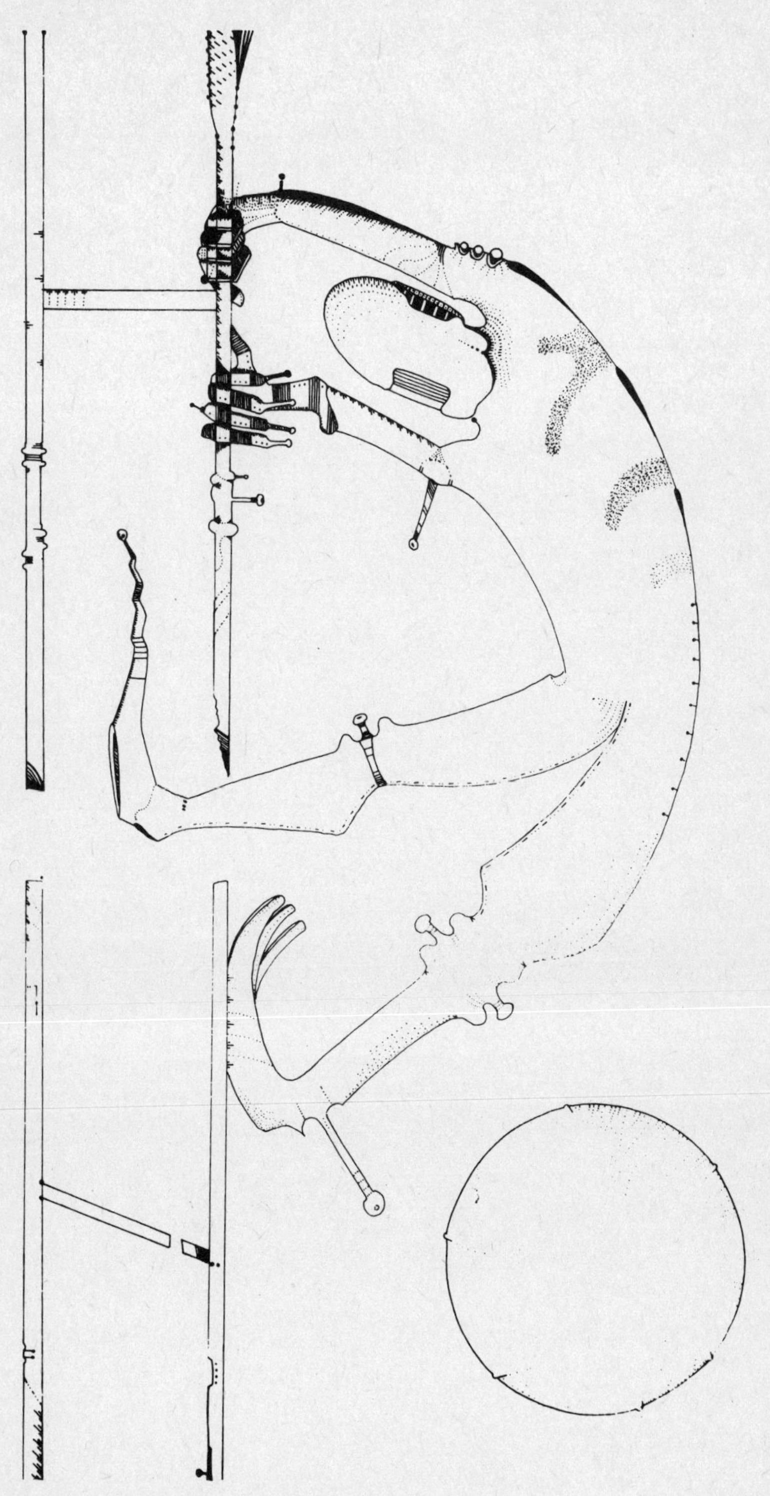

MODERN CATALAN POETRY

THE CATALAN LANDS

I

THE PLACE AND ITS CULTURE

To the stroller, Barcelona is a city of boulevards, sidewalk cafés, and small squares. During the late nineteenth century, Art Nouveau was popular with the rising Catalan bourgeoisie, and even the most staid residential blocks abound with surprises, sometimes grotesque, sometimes exquisite. Barcelona is Antoni Gaudi's town. His Güell Park, perched on one of the hills that ring the city, is one of the world's enchanted places — a play of fantasy that never overpowers the natural world it is meant to compliment. And from many spots one can see the Tibadado, an amusement park a little farther (and higher) from the center. Its sparkling strings of lights enhance the fairy tale atmosphere.

But there is another side to Barcelona too, one hardly mentioned until recently in Spanish and foreign newspapers. Workers killed and tortured, massive general strikes, a long campaign of cultural and political repression against the Catalan nation. In fact only now, with the death of Franco and the reestablishment of Catalan autonomy, is Barcelona again becoming what it was in the 1920's and 1930's: a flamboyant center of libertarian politics and social and artistic experimentation of every kind.

After a protracted period of silence, Catalan culture in general, and the printed word in particular, have been going through a period of renewal. Records in Catalan, often using works by poets like Salvador Espriu, Bartomeu Rosselló-Pòrcel and Miquel Martí i Pol as texts, rank high on the hit parade. *Today*, the first Catalan-language daily newspaper since 1939, has reached a circulation of seventy thousand. There are Catalan magazines of high intellectual content like *Serra d'Or* and reviews like *Oriflama* and *Cavall Fort* for adolescents and children. An excellent *Great Catalan Encyclopedia* is in the making, being issued volume by volume. It promises to be one of the finest works of its kind anywhere. On walls, on bumper stickers and on tee shirts one sees everywhere the affirmation that *"volem l'estatut"* ("we want the statute of autonomy"). In addition, there is now a thick catalogue of books in Catalan — history, technical works, translations of classical and modern authors (including Americans like Faulkner, Hemingway, and Nathaniel

West), literature, children's books — in short, the entire range of materials usually found on publishers' lists.

To understand the import of all this, a little historical background may be useful. Modern Spain has four major languages: Basque (which belongs neither to the Romance languages nor to any other language group), Castilian (what is usually called "Spanish"), Galician (the language of an area above Portugal), and Catalan. Catalan is spoken by about seven million people, some of whom live in the Balearic Islands, others in a small strip of southern France that includes Perpinyà, and others in Spain proper, from Alacant to the French border and between the Mediterranean Sea and Aragon. To take the Castilian contribution as *the* literature of Spain, either now or in the past, is to accept a myth propagated by the Spanish government and to miss about half the richness of Spanish writing.

The most interesting Catalan literature is of two periods: the medieval and early Renaissance (1250 to 1500), and the modern (approximately 1875 to the present). The first period produced several brilliant figures. One was Ramon Llull (ca. 1233-1316), a philosopher, poet, and storyteller who wrote in Arabic and Latin as well as Catalan. Another was Ausiàs March (ca. 1397-1459), a poet initially influenced by Dante and by the Occitan troubadours. March's own personality, however, led him towards a more stark and introspective verse.

March's poetry made effective use of the sound of Catalan — a rougher, brusquer sound than one usually finds in Romance languages. An example of the linguistic quality of Catalan would be these lines cited by Arthur Terry in *Catalan Literature*. They are followed by Jorge Montemayor's 1560 translation into Castilian and my own English:

Qui no e's trist, de mos dictats no cur,
o en algun temps que sia trist estat.

(No cure de mis versos, ni los lea
quien no fuese muy triste, o lo haya sido.)

(Let no one care for my words who isn't sad
or who hasn't been so at some time.)

Even those who know neither language will note the predominance of monosyllables and consonant endings in the Catalan.

March announced in one of his poems that he was *"lleixant a part l'estil dels trobadors"* ("leaving aside the troubadours' style"). He replaced it with a tortured literary personality that took him far beyond the conventions of courtly verse.

> *Colguen les gents   ab alegria festes,*
> *loant a Déu,   entremesclant deports;*
> *places, carrers,   e delitables horts*
> *sien cerquats   ab recont de grans gestes;*
> *e vaja yo   los sepulcres cerquant,*
> *interrogant   ànimes infernades,*
> *e respondran,   car no són companyades*
> *d'altre que mi   en son continu plant.*

> (Let the people   celebrate joyous holidays,
> praising God   and mingling sports;
> let squares, streets,   and delectable gardens
> be sought out   with songs of noble deeds,
> while I go out   in search of graves,
> questioning   the damned
> and they'll answer,   for I'm the only one
> who keeps them company   in their constant laments.)

Today March remains a strong influence on young Catalan poets, and his works continue to be widely read and sung. In fact, one of the newer poetry-publishing houses in Barcelona is called Ausiàs March Editions.

Another early figure worth mentioning is Joanot Martorell (ca. 1410-1468). A Valencian like March, Martorell has been called the first modern novelist. His greatest work, *Tirant lo Blanc,* was cited by Cervantes as "the best book in the world." Martorell has also had more recent admirers. The most prominent of them is Mario Vargas Llosa, a well-known Peruvian novelist who claims Martorell and Faulkner as his two main teachers. Martorell was an active knight, and his two favorite themes in *Tirant lo Blanc* are sex and political power in the Mediterranean. The realistic descriptions of warfare, the psychological depth of characterization, and the mixture of flowing prose and colloquial speech have made him a major figure in the history of European literature.

At the beginning of this early period, Catalonia was heavily influenced by the culture of Occitania. As time went on the Catalans developed separate traditions and modes of expression. Nonetheless Catalan, as a language, has always been closer to Occitan than to anything else. An example would be the word for bird: *pájaro* in Castilian, *oiseau* in French, *auzel* in Occitan, and *ocell* in Catalan. But the vitality and directness of the early Renaissance remain, at least in literature, far more alive in Catalonia than in Occitania. And these elements feed directly into the modern period. Indeed, poets in their twenties, like Ramon Pinyol, are still writing sonnets of love and revolution with caesuras in every line.

During the late 1800's, this continuity was nourished by the revival of the *Jocs Florals* (Floral Games), public poetry contests with their roots in the troubadour era. They came to play an important part in the life of Barcelona and of the Catalan Lands as a whole. For the last hundred years poets have had a special position there, acting as spokesmen for Catalan culture and political aspirations.

Between 1500 and 1800 Catalan life stagnated, both because of the shift of world trade from the Mediterranean to the Atlantic and because of series of civil wars in which Catalans took the losing side. But Catalonia was still the main center of Spanish commerce (as opposed to the shipment of gold through Seville). And with the beginnings of industrialization in the nineteenth century, the Catalans and the Basques were the first to build railroads, establish banks, and keep abreast of advances in Europe. At the same time Catalan, which had remained the spoken tongue but had nearly died out as a literary language, was taken up again by a group of intellectuals who were determined to make it an instrument of modern thought, and who also wanted political autonomy within Spain. They were supported in these endeavors by an important sector of the bourgeoisie. In the late nineteenth century Catalanist political parties were formed, Catalan newspapers and magazines were founded, and first-rate poets and novelists like Joan Maragall and Narcís Oller were published and encouraged.

The period from 1870 to 1939 was an intense and vital one in Catalonia. Industry developed rapidly. Barcelona spilled forth from its medieval walls and invaded the surrounding countryside. At the same time, anarchism took hold among the workers, producing such phenomena as a system of schools and lecture halls called Workers' Lyceums and later on Free Women, a radical feminist organization with a membership of twenty thousand. Theater groups, leftist organizations, newspapers and magazines flourished everywhere. Barcelona became one of the most exciting cities in Western Europe.

Along with the rise of avant-garde culture and radical politics, there was also a strong movement for Catalan autonomy. This movement, which was a response to the stagnation and conservatism of Madrid, reached its culmination in the Second Republic. During the 1930's Catalonia was a self-governing area with its own parliament and chief executive. Public signs and announcements were printed in Catalan and Castilian. A bilingual school system was created, and became one of the most progressive in the world. Catalan itself, as a language, was renovated and modernized – in particular by Pompeu Fabra, whose *General Dictionary of the Catalan Language* remains the standard one.

During the 1920's and 1930's, a number of outstanding poets appeared. Among them were J.V. Foix and Joan Salvat-Papasseit, experimentalists with one foot in surrealism and futurism, and the other in the medieval and Renaissance tradition. Their poetry is an unusual combination of whimsy and high seriousness, qualities that also coexist in the work of Joan Miró, Catalonia's most famous twentieth-century painter, and that until the Civil War seemed to be the special fingerprint of Catalan genius. The combination is still visible in a younger writer like "Miquel Desclot," whose poems bear such titles as "She, the Immortal Fairy, Appeared to Me Suddenly and with Her Harpoon of Lionbone Pierced My Drowsy Pupils." It is, to some extent, the spirit of architects like Gaudí, whose work mostly dates from the late nineteenth century. During the 1930's, also, a series of Catalan translations from the Greek and Roman classics appeared, Though mostly out of print since 1939, they remain the most comprehensive ever done in Spain. At the same time, a lively popular culture flourished in the local cabarets and theaters.

The victory of the fascists in 1939 brought all this to an end. Many of the most prominent intellectuals went into exile – some to

Latin America but most to France, where they lived through Hitler's invasion and the Vichy regime. Catalan was banned from public use, and large numbers of Catalan books were burned. Offices were hung with signs reading "Don't bark. Speak the language of the Spanish Empire." For writers who stayed behind, it was a time of pain and unreality. Catalonia's school system had been dismantled, and her language seemed in danger of becoming a dialect. No visitors came from abroad. Foreign periodicals were banned. The Spanish press, meanwhile, devoted itself to diatribes against the evils of Communism, separatism, and freemasonry. The twentieth century itself seemed to have been driven underground.

All of Spain was desperately poor in the years after the Civil War. Catalan children grew up not knowing how to read or write their native language. Businessmen made haste to appease the central government, speaking (as some of them had during the nineteenth century) a grotesque pidgin-Castilian that had the graces neither of that language nor of Catalan. Very slowly during the 1940's and 1950's, a few books — mostly Catalan classics of one sort or another — were reprinted for circulation in limited editions. But in the meantime a generation was growing up that had never known the trauma of the Civil War, or that remembered it only vaguely from childhood.

Then, in the 1960's, things began to change. Spain started to boom, developing and maintaining one of the world's highest industrial growth rates. New factories and blocks of flats sprang up in and around the big cities. Cheap labor from places like Aragon and Andalusia flooded into Catalonia, along with capital from Europe and the United States. In one decade the nation was transformed from something a bit less than it had been before the war into the largest industrial complex on the Mediterranean.

Today the overwhelming impression, as in northern Italy ten years ago, is of rapid and chaotic industrial expansion. Everywhere streets have been torn up and new buildings erected. Vast, bleak housing projects for workers rise on the outskirts of cities, often remaining without vital services such as schools and hospitals for several years. Cars and trucks, factories and power plants spew filth into the air, casting a permanent grey pall over the downtown sections. At the same time, in the stores and boutiques, in the wealthy suburbs, and in the daily life of Barcelona, Valencia, or Palma de Majorca, it is obvious that, more than ever before, there is *money* in Catalonia. Even the physical contrast between the healthier, taller young people and their elders is impressive. For it is now possible, as it was not for most people right after the war, to rear children on a diet that includes milk and meat as well as chickpeas and potato omelettes. For some people, indeed, Catalonia is a very profitable place. And the vast amount of tax evasion practiced by the rich — one of those public scandals nobody does anything about — makes it even more profitable.

At the base of all this prosperity are, on the one hand, the unskilled "immigrants" from the rest of Spain and, on the other, foreign capital. But the Catalan bourgeoisie (along with the Basque) has always been the most industrious in the land, and has been quick to take advantage of the opportunities offered. For them, also, this new-found wealth has meant an increase in self-confidence. And their sons and daughters at the universities of Barcelona and Valencia have embraced Catalanism even more enthusiastically than their elders. The essential justice of their cause is, to me, self-evident. At times, however, there are elements of race and class prejudice in their feelings. Most Catalans are not rich. They do, however, have a rather middle class way of looking at things. The industrial proletariat, on the other hand, is mostly composed of workers from other parts of Spain. In addition, Catalans are among the more "European-looking" Spaniards. Their coloration tends to be light, and they sometimes look upon other Spaniards much as Spaniards look upon Moroccans — as a semi-savage race somehwere between man and ape.

The Catalan economic boom has slackened recently, but the most immediate result of this slowing down has been a rise in political activity. Catalonia has been swept by strikes in the past three years. Its businessmen have emerged from their ostrich-like posture to complain about government discrimination, cultural repression, and the lack of basic human rights. In last year's election, eighty-five percent of the Catalan vote went to parties strongly favoring autonomy. Then, after a spectacular demonstration of at least a million people last September in Barcelona, this autonomy was reluctantly granted by the Madrid government. Many changes have already taken place, ranging in importance from bilingual street signs to the predominance of Catalan in the universities and the inauguration of all-Catalan radio stations.

There are, of course, many differences between the present and the 1930's. One interesting change is that Catalanism is far stronger now than it was then in Valencia and the Balearic Islands. In 1930 such areas were still provincial, semi-feudal societies, dominated by landowning classes heavily dependent on Madrid. Now they are far closer to the Principality (the four provinces of Barcelona, Girona, Lleida and Tarragona), and far more militant in their demands for autonomy and linguistic freedom.

In the past eighteen years Valencia, the Balearics, and the Principality have all undergone a cultural transformation. Literary exiles, including poets like "Pere Quart" (Joan Oliver) and Agusti Bartra, have returned. Restrictions on the publication of books have gradually eased. Writers like Salvador Espriu or Mercé Rodoreda, who were considered promising before 1939, have come into their own. And a number of completely postwar figures like Terenci Moix, a young experimental novelist, or poets such as Miquel Martí i Pol and Vicent Andrés Estellés have emerged. Joan Fuster, Joaquim Molas, and other critics have again tried to give Catalan writers a sense of their own special traditions and possibilities.

With Catalan culture again in the ascendant, this is a good moment to survey the poetry of the last sixty years. One of the most striking things about it — especially considering what a tight little world Catalonia is — is its diversity. From Brossa's crypticness to Bartra's long lined romanticism, from Foix's surrealism to Ferrater's directness, this book is full of the most varied visions and voices. It is this spectrum of styles and sensibilities, perhaps, that marks Catalan most clearly as a mature modern literature. The present anthology covers the period from approximately 1920 to the present. The first poet presented, Joan Salvat-Papasseit, died in 1924. The last two, Miquel Desclot and Ramon Pinyol, are themselves in their twenties. I have omitted poets such as Marià Manent and Carles Riba. It seems to me that their work belongs stylistically to what we would call either Romantic or symbolist verse.

Catalan poetry today is in good health, but its struggle to survive has been long and bitter. No other great modern literature has seen its basic means of expression so threatened. If Catalonia had succumbed to its fate as defined by the fascists, Catalan poets would have disappeared or turned into mummified vestiges of a dead culture. This, however, has not happened. Though at times forcibly

deprived of their audience, they have continuously produced work
of the highest level. Together, these poets have created a modern
literature in which volatile feelings, profuse and exuberant imagery,
and a deep sense of the literary past have all combined to produce a
dense accumulation of strong literary voices. I myself, as a poet, feel
that I have gained much from my close association with these writers
and their works. Under the constant threat of annihilation, they have
created a body of verse that is at once formally adventurous and
socially engeged, receptive to outside influences and yet secure in
its own national identity. One can only hope that these authors
will now be able to assume their rightful place in a nation at last
in control of its own destiny.

II

THE POETRY

For Catalan poetry, the late nineteenth and early twentieth
centuries were a period of feverish and concentrated development.
In 1850, the Catalan language was still an insignificant regional
dialect. By 1920 it had developed into a modern tongue with one
of the richest literatures in Europe. Though 1920 is the starting
point for this collection, a brief survey of nineteenth-century Catalan
verse will be of value here.

The beginning of the Catalan literary *renaixença* (renaissance)
is usually given as 1837. In that year Bonaventura Carles Aribau,
a middle class Catalan living in Madrid, published "To the Father-
land." Effectively and simply, Aribau's poem evoked the special
and intimate ties between a writer and his native tongue:

> *Si, quan me trobo sol, parl' amb mon esperit,*
> *en llemosi li parl' que llengua altra no sent,*
> *e ma boca llavors no sap mentir ni ment,*
> *puig surten mes raons del centre de mon pit.*

(If, when I'm alone, I speak with my spirit,
in Catalan I speak, for it hears no other language
and then my mouth cannot and does not lie
for my words rise up from the center of my breast.)

Aribau's successors, who organized and participated in the *Jocs Florals*, developed a poetry of nostalgic love for the Catalan countryside and history. Their work was generally modest in scope and ambition. Not until 1877 did a really major Catalan poet emerge. This was Jacint Verdaguer, a country priest whose two epics (*l'Atlàntida* and *Canigó*) galvanized Catalan literature into an expanded sense of its own possibilities. Vast in breadth and resonances, demanding in structure and vocabulary, Verdaguer's epics mark the first of several giant steps towards literary maturity. Thematically, *l'Atlàntida* is based on the revolt of the Titans, the destruction of Atlantis, and Columbus' discovery of America. The Pyrenees provide the setting for *Canigó*, which is the story of the victory of the Franks over the Moors and of Christianity over the pagan or fairy gods. With Verdaguer, nineteenth-century Catalan literature jumped from approximately nowhere up to the level of authors like Victor Hugo.

One immediate effect of Verdaguer's success was to inspire other young authors. Among these were the naturalistic novelist Narcís Oller and the playwright 'Angel Guimerà, both of whom produced works of European stature. One of Oller's greatest admirers was Émile Zola, who wrote the introduction to the French translation of his novel *The Butterfly*. Oller and Guimerà have been widely translated. They remain popular classics in the way Dickens and Shaw are in English. Verdaguer, Guimerà, and Oller represent the full flowering of the literary *renaizenca*. They were followed by a school known as Modernists. This group included the architect Antoni Gaudi, the painter and author Santiago Russinyol, and — in a vague way — the poet Joan Maragall.

Maragall's work, though only a few decades removed from Verdaguer's, is vastly different in tone and degree of sophistication. And accomplished translator of German authors like Goethe and Nietzsche, Maragall brought to his work a European literary sense beyond anything Verdaguer had possessed. Sensual, intimate, and also deeply concerned with public issues, Maragall's poetry establishes him as a major transitional figure between nineteenth and twentieth-century verse. Such qualities come together in a poem like "Paternal," written after an anarchist bombing in Barcelona:

Tornant del Liceu la nit
del 7 de novembre de 1893

Furient va esclatant l'odi per la terra,
regalen sang les colltorçades testes,
*   i cal anà' a les festes*
amb pit ben esforçat, com a la guerra.

A cada esclat mortal — la gent trèmula es gira:
la crudeltat que avança, — la por que s'enretira,
*   se van partint el món. . .*
Mirant el fill que mama,—la mare que sospira,
*   el pare arruga el front.*

*   Pro l'infant innocent,*
que deixa, satisfet, la buidada mamella,
*   se mira an ell, — se mira an ella,*
*   i riu bàrbarament.*

(Returning from the Liceu opera
house, the night of November 7, 1893

Raging hatred explodes through the land,
blood pours from heads on twisted necks,
        and to go out at night
you need a strong heart, as to a war.

At every mortal blast, the trembling people whirl.
The cruelty that advances, the fear that retreats,
        divide the world between them. . .
Seeing his son at the breast, and the sighing mother,
        the father wrinkles his brow.

        But the innocent child
who satisfied, releases the emptied nipple,
        stares at him, stares at her,
        and laughs barbarously.)

The groundwork for modern Catalan poetry was completed by two Majorcan poets (Joan Alcover and Miquel Costa i Llobera) and the critic Eugeni d'Ors. D'Ors and his followers, collectively known as *noucentistes* (twentieth-centuryists), broke with the individualistic Romanticism of Maragall and his contemporaries. Instead, writers like Josep Carner, "Guerau de Liost," and Carles Riba developed a poetry of aesthetic distance, irony, and a new kind of attention to form. Such poetry consciously attempted to recoup Catalan literature's lost centuries of development and to reestablish contact with Renaissance humanism — a tradition felt to have been broken off after the time of Ausiàs March. *Noucentisme* was essential to putting a final polish of culture and formal flexibility on Catalan verse.

Modern Catalan poetry begins after 1915, when one begins to find a new combination of stylistic freedom and direct speech. Although quite different in many ways, both Joan Salvat-Papasseit and J.V. Foix reveal this combination. Both poets felt the liberating influence of the futurist and surrealist schools. Salvat, in poems like "Drama in the Port" and "Marseille, Port d'Amour," makes use of Apollinaire's visual experiments. Salvat's work also reveals the influence of Marinetti and the futurists — particularly in his fascinated descriptions of Barcelona's cranes, ships, and streetcars, Such influences, however, are relatively superficial. What really is of interest in Salvat's work is the concrete, detail-packed imagery and the conversational tone. In place of "literary tradition," one finds a passion for popular culture — songs, circuses, Charlie Chaplin — and a sometimes poignant, sometimes joyous love affair with the physical and social universe around him. Bartomeu Rosselló-Pòrcel, in "Bridge at Twilight," explicitly acknowledges Appolinaire's importance for a whole generation of Catalan poets. What all these writers had in common with the French poet was an essential gaiety of vision and a will to embrace the world as it is.

Along with Salvat, J. V. Foix is the other major Catalan poet of the 1920's. In an early sonnet like "I Fear the Night," one can see traces of the *noucentistes,* of the nineteenth-century symbolists, and of medieval and Renaissance authors like Guido Cavalcanti and Francis Petrarch. Deeply conscious of a specifically Mediterranean cultural tradition, Foix attempts to reaffirm classical values in the face of a violent and chaotic twentieth century. His poems often comment indirectly on political events. "At the Entrance. . .," for example, responds to the brutal beginnings of the Spanish Civil War. "I Arrived in that Town. . .," ŏne of his finest works, expresses the sense of disorientation that came over many Catalans after 1939.

Foix's attitude towards modern life is somewhat more ambivalent than Salvat's. "At the Foot of a Cyclopean Wall. . ." celebrates the mechanical world of airplanes and industrial draftsmen, but it also links this world to pagan Mediterranean traditions and the "Eternal Ungraspable." In his efforts to reunite a fragmented world through a search for meaningful cultural roots, Foix is close both to Eugeni d'Ors' programmatic humanism and to such North American figures as T.S. Eliot and Ezra Pound.

In Catalonia, as in all of Europe, the 1930's were a time of increased political commitment among poets. At the forefront of the movement towards revolutionary verse in Catalonia were Pere Quart and, a few years later, Agustí Bartra. Quart, in a poem like "Useless Stars, Useless Bell" or in the postwar "Paid Vacation," balances direct political statement against an exuberantly surrealistic imagination. In part, both of these poems are attacks on public indifference and passivity. "Paid Vacation," however, strikes much closer to home. Its target is the cowed and obedient bourgeoisie of the 1940's. Quart's language is brusque and direct, often edged with self-mockery. Though this is perhaps his most typical tone, he can evoke a wide range of moods, ranging from the whimsy of pieces like "Pig" from his *Bestiary* to the bittersweet nostalgia of "Songs of Exile," written shortly after the Civil War.

Like Quart, Bartra can be both declamatory and lyrical. His Whitman-influenced "Many" is one of the finest poems to come out of the Spanish Civil War. "Many" is Whitmanesque in more than style. Something that has made Whitman a difficult poet for twentieth-century North American authors to assimilate is his deep identification with the United States. This quality of national rapport is one of the distinguishing features of Catalan verse. Most of the authors in this anthology identify strongly – though at times angrily – with the Catalan nation. Their sense of deep and intimate solidarity, along with the feeling that poets are national spokesmen (as they have been in Ireland, another colonized European nation) is one main source of the energy of Catalan verse.

If a certain joyous flamboyance marks poems like Salvat's "Wedding March" or Rosselló-Pòrcel's "Bridge at Twilight," bitterness and irony are the characteristic tones of the postwar. One can find them in poems like Brossa's "Defeat" or Quart's "Paid Vacation," and they are particularly pervasive in the work of Salvador Espriu. Silence, death, a revulsion against the ugliness and sterility of postwar life dominate Espiru's work. In "Suburban Square" the poet, "chattering away/ to myself in Catalan/ defunct language of funeral chants," stands in contrast to a world of censored films, hurdy-gurdies, and public drunkeness. In defeated Catalonia, the poet has become "a one-eyed man," king among the blind subjects of a totalitarian state. Yet for all this, Espriu in "Trial Hymn in the Temple," one of his most famous poems, still loves "with a desperate grief,/ this my poor/ dirty, sad, unlucky homeland." Silence and death are also psychological themes for Espriu, and seem to be the coordinates of his private sensibility: a dark and anguished lyricism that finds its echo in the external world.

Though all three of them make good use of the breakthroughs of the 1920's, Quart, Bartra, and Espriu all have too much to say to worry about experimentation for its own sake. With Brossa and Estellés, however, we re-enter the world of the avant-garde. Brossa's interest in theater and the visual arts is apparent in works like "The Kiss" and "Poem with Black Background." Estellés, the second enentirely postwar figure in this collection, has certain stylistic affinities with Andalusian poets like Federico Garcia Lorca. Part of the affinity lies in Estellés' dominant imagery: a world of interpenetrating violence, sexuality, and nature. Although one does not wish to push the idea too far, it is intriguing to note that Estellés is indeed from a lusher, more passionate area often described as the Catalan Andalusia.

Estellés is the first major postwar poet in this book. The Principality, however, has also produced at least two outstanding poets since 1950: Gabriel Ferrater and Miquel Martí i Pol. Ferrater's career was cut short by his suicide in 1972. In the twelve years preceding his death, his poetic impact was tremendous. Less rhetorical then any major poet since Salvat, Ferrater's work at first glance seems entirely natural and intimate. Actually, he was both better-read and more in control of his materials than Salvat had been. Although "naturalness" is always something of an illusion in literature, Ferrater's determination to make Catalan speech-rhythms the basis of his poetic language influenced a number of younger writers. Its fiercely concentrated imagery keeps his verse from falling into prosaicness.

Martí i Pol — though in a somewhat different fashion — also uses everyday speech as a source of poetry. Much of his work centers around Roda de Ter, a small factory town where he grew up and still lives. A local poet in the same sense that Miró described himself as an "international Catalan," Martí i Pol uses Roda de Ter to tell us a good deal about Spain, the world, and life in general. A poem like "In Memoriam," for example, is really about the tragic consequences of the Civil War for all Spaniards. Another, "Nocturne," concentrates in a few lines all the bleakness, ugliness, and hard work of industrial life. What comes through Martí i Pol's work, however, is not so much despair as a deep identification with the lives and sufferings of ordinary people. In the imagery of nature and daily routine in "Summer," he finds — despite "the effort and the monotony of work and life" — eternal patterns of creativity, love, and self-renewal.

With Francesc Parcerisas, we move into a more recent generation. In his work English and North American influences, surrealism, and an increased sexual openness blend into a personal vision more confident and joyous than anything since 1939. Both Parcerisas and Marta Pessarrodona have taught in England, and the experience has affected both as poets. But whereas Parcerisas is often whimsical, Pessarrodona's work is more likely to be tough and bitter. She has cultivated a hard-boiled, cynical speaking voice that, paradoxically, often reveals an intense vulnerability. "The Cruelty of the Months," a poem inspired by the death of Gabriel Ferrater, comes the closest of any in this book to centering on the poet's private anguish.

I have included the two final poets, Ramon Pinyol and Miquel Desclot, in order to give some idea of what the youngest Catalans are writing. Pinyol's work with sonnets is typical of much that has been written during the past few years. In part, he and other poets like him represent a turning away from the techniques of figures like Ferrater and Martí i Pol and a determination to see what kinds of resources fixed forms still can offer. Just as typical, however, is Desclot, whose long titles inevitably bring to mind J.V. Foix and whose work in general continues the explorations of the avant-garde.

A selection of this kind can offer little more than an introduction to the literature it represents. Many of these poets certainly deserve separate volumes in English. What I hope I have suggested, however, is the extraordinary range and vitality of modern Catalan verse. When one thinks that so much outstanding poetry has come from a nation of only seven million, many of whom have been prevented from learning to read and write their language, it really is astonishing. The usual banalities of dialect and "regional" literature are conspicuous by their absence. Instead one finds a mixture of high sophistication, receptiveness to international experimentation, and a deep rootedness in the Catalan nation. I hope that this anthology may begin to make North Americans in general — and poets in particular — aware of one of the finest modern literatures in Europe.

David H. Rosenthal
Barcelona-New York, 1974-1978

EDITOR'S NOTE

As much as possible, I have used standard English place-names in this book, for example *Iviza*, not the Catalan *Eivissa* or Castilian *Ibiza*. All other place names have been rendered in their Catalan forms, and not in Castilian, for example *Alacant*, not *Alicante*.

MODERN CATALAN POETRY

Picasso
25.7.61.

JOAN SALVAT-PAPASSEIT

(1894-1924)

Salvat-Papasseit is one of the few Catalan poets with a working class background. His father, a stoker on the steamship *Montevideo*, died in 1901, and Salvat spent most of his childhood in a charity home. In 1914 he began publishing revolutionary political essays in two Castilian-language magazines: *Social Justice* and *The Wretched Ones*. Two years later Salvat switched to Catalan, and in 1917 he founded the political-cultural journal *An Enemy of the People: Cultural Subversion Sheet*. In 1919 the first of his six volumes of poetry appeared. A year later he found that he had tuberculosis, and the remainder of his poetic career was overshadowed by his impending death.

Salvat emerged as a writer during one of Barcelona's most exciting periods, a time of anarchist strikes and manifestoes, burgeoning Catalan nationalism, and intense receptivity to every kind of new political and artistic theory. He himself was drawn to the futurists, and their influence can be seen in some of the poems included here. What makes him so engaging to us, however, is his vivid sense of life in Barcelona's poorer quarters — in particular Barceloneta, a neighborhood of fishermen and small artisans that faces the Mediterranean. The taste and smell of the harbor, the detailed texture of everyday existence, are central to the continuing delight of Salvat's poetry.

DRAMA IN THE PORT

to Lluis Escobet

SLOSH OF OCEAN
        IN THE NIGHT
(CLOTHED IN THE LIGHT OF MEN

                V O L T A I C ‑ A R C)

AT MY FEET
        WHITE LIGHTS
                GREEN
                      RED

THE T R A N S A T L A N T I C MALE

HOWLING

THE SIRENS DON'T KNOW IT
                BUT THEY SHRIEK
THE EMIGRANTS SHOVE
      I WALK TOWARDS THE D R E D G E
                WHICH IS DARK AND RISES
THE UNEASY BUOY
         H A W V
        E D A E

NOW THE WAVES SING THEIR URGE TO DEVOUR

THE THUNDER   FAR-OFF
                SIGH OF DARKNESS
I SEE MYSELF IN THE HORIZON

BEYOND THE HARBOR THE SEAGULLS REST

To J.V. Foix

The turning dynamo moves its fiery members
      in CIRCUMVOLUTION
I've never seen more majesty than in this pen of fire
TROLLEY   TROLLEY   TROLLEY
For I am the equal of anyone
             in this alley
It makes you sick   everyone knows some foreign language
    and surely this old man doesn't know my name

Another wears eyeglasses
          with dirty lenses
Against his nose   Against his nose
    BECAUSE THE TICKET INSPECTOR

The conductor had the floor before
      (and winked at me:
      5-4-0-4-5)

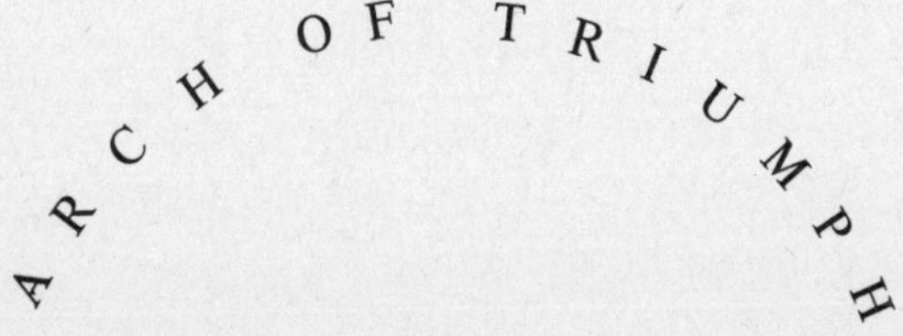

I searched myself furiously
          if they've taken my wallet
In truth I didn't have one   friend

MAP

To J. M. de Sucre

AVENTINE MOUNT

<pre>
        D
        E
        C
        A
        D
        E
        N
        C
        E   C H U R C H
                                     E
                                      S
COTTAGES

        ARISTOCRACY   V I C E
        I R O N Y I N C R I M E

                                    S
                                    U
                                    B
                                    U
                                    R
                                    B
                                    S

  H   POOR WHORES
    O   A L   THE GALLEY
      S P I T   HONESTY   HUNGER
</pre>

The sun ignites everything
— without consuming it

LINOLEUM

To Xenius

I've just embarked
                  in a Hindu longboat
(Write to me in the Far-West

I profit from it all
to kill my family's memories of me)

Now that my woman sleeps confidingly
And my little son to come
      And they won't line up
                 like others
                     at the bakery

And a star still burns
     and I carry my tomahawk under my arm

A used book-seller
           walks past
                swinging the Poems
                     every one of Them unpublished

— I really can't leave
     without first strangling that bookseller

INTERIOR

To J. Carbonell i Gener

We're seated
        around the table
        near the whistling gaslight

Some artificial flowers
    which bring me pain
               because they never feel the winter

The eyes of my beloved
           gleam like a cat's

Or like fish-scales

The room's windowpanes shake
    resound with the jolting of trams

The wooden mannequin
           seems like a specter

Just now I knocked over the inkwell with my arm

    The dark spot spread
and as superstition makes its entrance
WE'VE GROWN PALE

CHRISTMAS

I feel the cold of night
                    and the dark holiday drúms.
Like the group of young men who go by now singing.
I hear the celery cart
               that the pavement supports
and the others who push it, making straight for the market.

Those at home   in the kitchen,
                      near the burning coal-stove
with the gaslights turned up have prepared the cock.
Now I gaze at the moon, which seems full;
and they gather up the feathers,
                     already longing for tomorrow.

Tomorrow at our table we'll forget the poor
— as poor as we are —.
              By then Christ will have been born.
He'll glance our way during dessert
and when he sees us   he'll break into tears.

I SING OF BATTLE

Cavalier on his steed
             with flaming mane
that's me setting adolescent words on fire
I curse the gods in full flight:
      the cringing herd
           fears the whip of my song!
And I've married the moon
(But I don't sleep with Her if philistines govern my domains).

"oh viens tout près de moi
puis pose avec émoi
tes lèvres sur ma bouche
— dans un baiser farouche
je serai toute à toi!

I will kiss her
as she should be
kissed

A GIRL PRAYS IN MY VESSEL :

a little sailor who's not watchful — a pirate comes

he brought her no song — a pirate comes and takes his love

BENEATH THE SAILS I WILL TAKE HER

and steals his beloved

MARSEILLE PORT D'AMOUR

NOTRE DAME DE LA GARDE PRIEZ POUR NOUS

PASSION IN THE METRO

(REFLEX No. 1)

To Joaquim Borralleras

Antinoüs   young lord of Priapus lost
and a rose in his lips to guide him in the night

His eyes shine so
that Penelope unrobes
and her face languishes like a wax virgin

Antinoüs is in the dark   and a rose in his lips
that wants to do her villainy
                              to charm Penelope
                              the untamed

Antinoüs has slowly
                eaten
        A   R O S E

*—written while passing beneath the Seine's snake on the
Saint-Lazare line*

LA FEMME AUX ORANGES

(REFLEX No. 2)

The metro's song at the old Cité, which bathes its belly
in the Seine, oozes through all the roofs and says:

> — Today I'm perfumed
> with printed grease.
> I wear a blue bracelet,
> another of scarlet
> and my hips quite naked.
>
> My sandals bright with diamonds.
>
> And so my beloved
> comes unspeakably sought-after
> and descends to Rennes
> leaving her girdle at Saint-Michel
> and lies down in my bath of purple.
>
> Bath of the NORTH-SOUTH line!

The song ended when la femme aux oranges, going towards
Château d'Eau, opened her blouse and showed her nipples
                    which were like smoking oil-lamps

Paris, March 12, 1920

MARXA NUPCIAL

Llum de l'**IRRADIADOR** camaleònic damunt
l'estrella del <u>Circ</u> encara hexagonal

    Exit!   Exit!!   Exit!!!

CLOWNS equilàters   líders romàntics
Això és sa   i en les constel·lacions de quatre barrets
cònics

La terra només gira perquè jo sóc aquí i jo sóc un
PALLASSO qui agonitza

Margot amb el **MALLOT** i els cabells pintats
rojos sembla un ciri que cremi
Només crema per mi:
Davant dels cent centaures que fan faixa a la Pista
<u>**DAURADA D'EMOCIÓ**</u>

Margot ara m'esguarda fit a fit   i en caient del
Trapezi he llegit un <u>anunci</u> a la pantalla:

———————————————————————

Escopiu a la closca
pelada
        dels cretins

———————————————————————

WEDDING MARCH

Light of the chameleon **RADIANCE** above
the star of the <u>Circus</u> still hexagonal

    Success!   Success!!   Success!!!

equilateral **CLOWNS**   romantic leaders
This is healthy   and in the constellations of four conical
hats

The earth only turns because I am here and I am a
CLOWN in agony

Margot with the **TIGHTS** and her hair painted
red seems like a burning candle
She only burns for me:
Before the hundred centaurs that form a barrier in the arena
<u>**GILDED WITH EMOTION**</u>

Margot stares at me now   and in falling from the
Trapeze I read an <u>advertisement</u> on the screen:

**SPIT ON THE BALD
PATE**

OF THE CRETINS

Aquest home que diu:
—La música de <u>Circ</u> és tan definitiva com no lo va conèixer
Richard Wagner   tanmateix un pompier!

La sombra dels comparses en el sol de les taules
Moure's   i projectar-se   no existir:
La   **VIDA**   al Dinamisme
Jo protesto que això degeneri també
—Perquè ara el "domador" vol fer jocs malabars
i els cavalls   amb les potes

Més m'estimo l'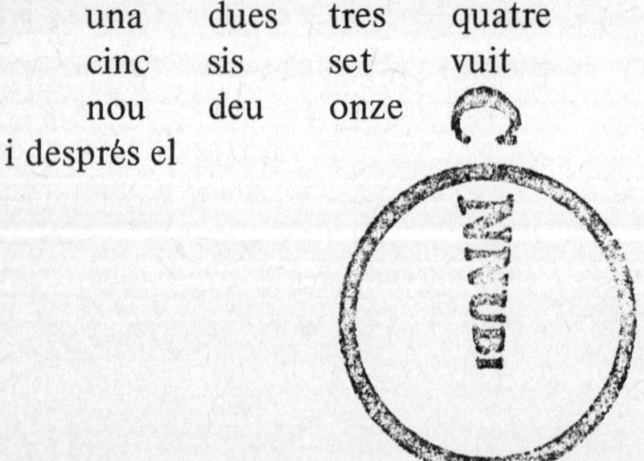

i en   **ChaRLoT**   que s'han tornat bessons per
tal d'entrar en sèrio a la glòria del cel

(car ells són ignorants de que venim d'ahir
d'abans d'ahir   de l'altre abans d'ahir
        i més d'abans encara)

L'Esfera del rellotge a les **DOTZE** fecunda les hores
que vindran   que són:

        una   dues   tres   quatre
        cinc   sis   set   vuit
        nou   deu   onze
i després el

—i aixt seré immortal perquè d'aquí ha nascut el meu
JO dins el **TOT**

This man who says:
"Circus music is more definitive than anything Richard
Wagner knew of"   a fireman notwithstanding!

The shadow of masquerades in the sun of the tables
To move   and project yourself   not to exist:
LIFE   in Dynamism
I protest that this also may degenerate
— Because now the "tamer" wants to juggle
and the horses   with their hoofs

I prefer   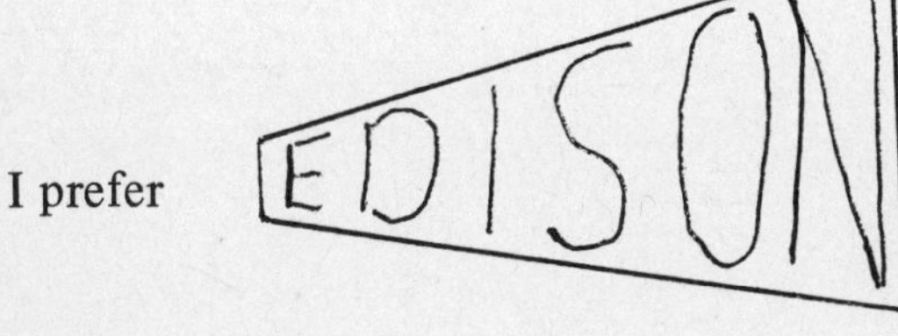

and CHARLIE CHAPLIN who have become twins in hope of
seriously entering the glory of heaven

(since they don't know that we come from yesterday
from the day before yesterday   from before the day before yesterday
          and from even before)

The Dial of the clock at TWELVE engenders the hours
to come   which are:

     one   two   three   four
     five   six   seven   eight
     nine   ten   eleven

and then

— and so I shall be immortal because here was born my
I in EVERYTHING

EPIGRAM

To Josep Font i Cases

A perfume of colors invaded Margot
She dressed quickly:
Lest anyone know the scent of her breasts
she placed a flower
                    on her fresh clothes

J. V. FOIX

(1894-   )

At eighty-four, Foix remains the acknowledged master of avant-garde Catalan poetry. Since 1917 he has been closely associated with the nation's artistic vanguard, including internationally known painters like Joan Miró and Salvador Dali, both of whom he presented in their first one-man Barcelona shows. In the course of his long career, Foix has edited magazines like *The Catalan Review, Pieces,* and *Monitor,* and has contributed to many other publications. During parts of the 1920's and 1930's, he directed the cultural section of the Barcelona daily newspaper *Publicity.* He represented Catalonia at the 1934 PEN Club conference in Dubrovnik. In addition to his cultural activities, Foix is also the prosperous owner of two fine pastryshops. His customers sometimes ask him if by any chance he has a son who writes those far-out poems with the long titles.

Though Foix denies being a surrealist, the movement is obviously one factor in his work. Equally important, however, are his feeling for the Catalan past and landscape — its sailors and shepherds, mountains and sea — and his deeply sensual imagery. Foix is immersed in the medieval and Renaissance Mediterranean poetic tradition — the tradition of the troubadours, of Guido Cavalcanti and Dante, of Ramon Llull and Ausiàs March. He often uses these sources in counterpoint with the more experimental side of his work. The combination of elements in his verse, along with his sure lyric sense, make him a major figure in contemporary European poetry.

I fear the night, but night transports me,
Rigid, down lanes past the sooty sea;
In the dying light the street-band is heard, dischordant,
I'm alone with myself, and this comforts me.

Black coals ring the dead sea,
The low hill and the pine slope,
But in them I see a dense jungle
And imagine a door in the barren desert.

The dark night seems a blackboard
And like a child, I draw strange heads on it,
A brand-new world and the land that desire tells.

I marvel, and am afraid — oh night that sharpens
Stars and wisdom! — You fill the sea with clothes,
And a voice says: "It's raining blood in the catch-basins."

IT WAS GETTING DARK AND WE WERE
LOOKING AT THE SKINS SCATTERED AROUND
THE SADDLE-MAKER'S HOUSE

Already vapors clothe the gardens;
The roots, in earth and walls, retire into mystery.
Both, discarded leather effigies
In the night's dark sandpit,
We yield, fraternal, to the fraudulent hour.
Excited, the mares in their herds,
Born in shadow and on shadow nourished,
Reach the hamlets.
Above the sky's elephant skin
Stars open their airy paths.

Si poqués acordar Raó i Follia,
I en clar matí, no lluny de la mar clara,
La meva ment, que de goig és avara,
Em fes present l'Etern, I amb fantasia

—Que el cor encén i el meu neguit desvia—
De mots, de sons i tons, adesiara
Fes permanent l'avui, i l'ombra rara
Que m'estrafà pels murs, fos seny i guia

Del meu errar per tomarius i lloses;
—Oh dolços pensaments!, dolçors en boca!—
Tornessin ver l'Abscon, i en cales closes

Les imatges del son que l'ull evoca,
Vivents; i el Temps no fos; i l'esperança
En Immortals Absents, fos llum i dansa!

If I could reconcile Reason and Madness
And in clear morning, not far from clear sea
My mind, avaricious for joy,
Could make the Eternal present. And with Fantasy

—That the heart inflames and my uneasiness turns aside —
Of words, sounds, and tones, could
Occasionally make today permanent, and that strange shadow
That mimicked me on walls, be good sense and guide

For my wanderings among tamarisks and tombstones;
— Oh sweet thoughts! Sweetness in mouth! —
They might make the Secret true, and in sheltered inlets

Bring alive sleep's eye-evoked images;
And Time might not be; and the hope
Of Absent Immortals, light and dancing!

AT THE FOOT OF A CYCLOPEAN WALL, THE MAN IN THE BLUE WORKSUIT, TALLEST OF ALL, WAS POLISHING LEATHER STRAPS AND ADJUSTING PULLEYS. FROM TIME TO TIME HE LOOKED AT ME FROM BENEATH HIS STRANGE VISOR, TACITURN. I PRETENDED NOT TO NOTICE, WHILE WATCHING THE SEA WITH AN OLD BOOK IN MY HAND

In fable and sleep I know that man who,
Among ancient rocks near the open sea,
Scatters fake faded stars covered with printed sheets.
Torch in hand, I've followed him among twin-engine planes
When in secret he anoints their gears
In elliptical hangars and sacred watch-posts.
I've seen him, regal, in a cave of the sea
As if dressed in moss
Beneath a stifling sun
          — when the hand-shaped shadows
Retire into streams and see births —
Or within a closed wall
          — when the hours anchor
In mental harbors —
          humming and surrounded by tools,
Measuring stellar chasms and their foliage.

It's the menhir of forested dawn
Rustling with waterflowers and scented light,
Muscle, adolescent and bloody, of midday,
Bird of the afternoon, exiled
Among wandering propellers, mortal,
And evanescent motors, on the captive runway.
Night's androgyne, generous with seed,
Darkening the solitudes of primitive meadows,
Present wherever we covet the body,
Perennial flame on the battlements of calm,
A singing breeze in the leafy blueness,
Ancestral form in the nocturnes of inlets,
Brightness of ash-trees in the passages of dreams.

It's the Eternal Ungraspable wandering through dunes:
"Light on your face when you see me and grow silent."
Or it pierces the boulders with impalpable drills:
"It opens vast vistas above scarlet seas
when the night-fishing boats set sail from port
and deep humid voices modulate their chants."
It invokes new gods on the abstract beaches:
"Your name exalted by gay northwinds
when joy runs to seed you faint and you pray."
Immortal burning speck in the ocean's ravines:
"Your body bursts forth in unseen leaves and flowers."
It bears secret creatures in immanent groves:
"When the shadow of both is the Single Shadow."

1935

AT THE ENTRANCE TO AN UNDERGROUND
STATION, BOUND HAND AND FOOT BY
BEARDED CUSTOMS OFFICIALS, I SAW HOW
MARTA SET OFF IN A TRAIN FOR THE
FRONTIER. I WANTED TO SMILE AT HER,
BUT A POLICELIKE MILITIAMAN CARRIED
ME OFF WITH HIS OWN FAMILY, AND SET
FIRE TO THE WOODS

Stairs of glass on the solar platform
Where trains of light leave for open beaches
Among transparent walls and branching corals
And bright-eyed birds in branches' buzzing.

Is it you, white in the white of this insular dawn,
— Liquid of gaze, hearing inner music —
Do you write wet goodbyes on the forest of windowpanes,
With seed of night for an open dream?

You go beyond joy towards enchanted shores
With gigantic drunks in the thorny cove
And dissected falcons on rocks marked with crosses,
To a see where gods walk in night's furtive onset.

I can't reach you, sleeping, blind to light and in mind,
Dressed like a child, without voice or supplies,
Guarded among hoes by double-formed innkeepers;
The passports are old and bloody the hearts.

You take mountains and rivers and stellar lakes
And fountains in cool shadows in deep mailsacks;
A shadowy watch from the flaming peak
Calls to me with strange names and says no with his hands.

In the open they wave torn flags.

September, 1936

WHEN I SLEEP, THEN I SEE CLEARLY

to Joana Givanel

When it rains I dance alone
Dressed in algae, gold, and fishscales.
There's a stretch of sea at the turning
And a piece of scarlet sky.
A bird whirls in flight
And a bush brings forth branches,
The pirate's old mansion
Is a broad sunflower.
When it rains I dance alone
Dressed in algae, gold, and fishscales.

When I laugh I look hunchbacked
In the pool beneath the threshing floor.
I dress like an old gentleman,
I chase the custodian's wife,
And between pinegrove and oak
I plant my flag;
With a sack-needle I kill
The monster I never name.
When I laugh I look hunchbacked
In the pool beneath the threshing floor.

When I sleep, then I see clearly
Maddened by sweet poison
With pearls in both hands
I live in a shellfish's heart,
I'm a fountain on the canyon floor
And a wild beast's bed,
— Or the waning moon
As it dies beyond the ridge.
When I sleep, then I see clearly
Maddened by sweet poison.

April, 1939

MY COUNTRY'S A ROCK . . .

To the family line of the
Foixes and the Torrents

My country's a rock
Bearing leaves, flowering, seeding.
Freed from hunting, I keep a shed there
Without pallet or logs.
With no elms or pinegroves,
And the night goes to roost, cold
Without heather or brush.
The sky conquers weariness
And if the moon grows slender,
I pasture the docile eagle-owl.

I make my bed of silence
With a headboard of fogs.
Winds from high passes tuck me
Among rock-slope branches.
Everything wings, advancing, pure,
Down paths of liberation
When sleep lights the summit.
I'm the shepherd in a place
Where time has no plumb-lines
Nor man darts for crime.

I don't need folds or snares,
And I've got a milking shed.
Beneath groves of ice and air
I drink the ponds' salt.
On sunned and shaded slopes
I'm the last of my race
With mesas to all winds.
They're all there, without mystery,
Beneath captive crosses
In a delta of streams.

Freedmen, tough, with freeheld land,
In a circle compass points their slingshot
Smote the centuries' menhir
In an autumn of oxen.
Oh, the pure honeys of that spot!
Rediscovering my people's image
Water beyond the furtive garden,
Wet with dew from the cavern,
Eternal night's heirs
With the stars for hot ashes!

If among peaks my mind pains me,
Dawn's flowers perfume me
With broad dells' brightnesses.
I'm the stone in forgiving calm,
Fixed in a miraculous throat,
Everyone's oracle, and my own.
I come and go from rock to rock
— Or I pasture shaved pebbles
In a woods of confused cries —
And when it's dark, I fan the fire.

Els Torrents de Lladurs, August, 1939

**I ARRIVED IN THAT TOWN, EVERYONE
GREETED ME AND I KNEW NO ONE; WHEN
I WAS GOING TO READ MY VERSES, THE
DEVIL, HIDDEN BEHIND A TREE, CALLED
OUT TO ME SARCASTICALLY, AND FILLED
MY HANDS WITH NEWSPAPER CLIPPINGS**

What's the name of this town
With flowers on the steeple
And a river with dark trees?
Where did I leave my keys?

Everyone says "Good morning!"
I go around half-dressed;
Some people are kneeling,
Another gives me his hand.

"What's my name?" I ask them.
I look at my bare foot;
In the shadow of a barrel
A puddle of blood is shining.

The cowherd lends me a book,
I see myself in a window;
My beard has gotten long.
—What's become of my apron?

Such crowds there are in the square!
They're probably waiting for me;
I, who read them verses;
They're laughing as they leave.

The bishop decorates me,
The musicians have already stopped;
I'd like to go home,
But I don't know the side-streets.

If a girl kissed me. . .
What would my job be then?
Now the doors close.
Who knows where the pension is!

On a bit of newspaper
My portrait flutters;
The trees in the square
Wave goodbye to me.

What do they say on the radio?
I'm cold, I'm scared, I'm hungry;
I'll buy him a watch.
What's his Saint's Day?

I'm going to Font Vella.
They've pulled up the benches;
Now I see the Devil
Who awaits me around the corner.

September, 1942

WE WERE THREE, WE WERE TWO, IT WAS ME ALONE, WE WERE NONE . . .

To Rosa Leveroni

We were three, our heads down, in the darkness of vintages,
With the sea in our eyes and wine-dregs on our hands,
When the canal starts smoking in the forest's salt
And a child's cry sparkles upon the mountain.

We were two, standing on the rock of stars,
Our hearts bloody, without darts or sling,
When the wasteland starts burning and the tar begins to sob
In the latent deeps of lighthouse furrows.

It was me alone, a shade among old shadows,
Representing another shadow, on the beach
Where, among spread nets, the sleep of all
Signs on in the feverish darkness.

We were none, robed in leaves of darkness
When fear rains on the petals of marshes
And the other, the Pure, freed from rudder and sails
Sets out, watchfully, towards the brilliant Instant.

Port Lligat, August, 1953

BARTOMEU ROSSELLÓ-PÒRCEL

(1913-1938)

Rosselló-Pòrcel was born in Palma de Majorca. When he died of tuberculosis in 1938, he was considered one of the most promising young Catalan poets. Altogether, three books of his poems were published (one posthumously), as well as translations of André Gide and C. F. Ramuz' *Histoire d'un soldat.*

One of the four poems included here ("For Majorca, During the Civil War") has practically become that island's national anthem. It's a kind of poem that sometimes loses in translation, but any reader should be able to feel Rosselló's love of his homeland's clear air and bright mountain ranges. The poem was written in 1937, shortly before his death in a sanitorium. In recent years, Rosselló.Pòrcel's work has gained a wider audience through the efforts of Maria del Mar Bonet, a Majorcan folksinger who has set many of his works to music and recorded them.

BRIDGE AT TWILIGHT

Les feux rouges des ponts . . .
— Apollinaire

The lofty night and I
embrace — all alone in the streets.
The lanterns of little squares
    pursue us.

The burnt houses, black,
and in front of bordellos, with blouses
of June wind, adventure:
    Madame Clara and Madame Barbara.

In the doorways, bandits
fearful of me, who don't venture out.

The sun on the rooftops
    dances
with a stunningly beautiful girl.

FOR MAJORCA, DURING THE CIVIL WAR

Those fields still turn green,
those groves remain,
and my mountains are etched
above the same azure.
The stones always invoke
the difficult rain, the blue rain
that comes from you, bright ridge,
my mountains, pleasure, brightness!
I'm greedy for the light, lingering in my eyes,
that makes me tremble when I remember you!
Now the gardens are like music;
they trouble and tire me like some slow tedium.
Autumn's heart already fades
fixed with delicate smoke-clouds.
And the grass turns brown on hunting party
hills, among September dreams
and dusk-tinted fogs.

All my life is bound to you,
like flames at night to the darkness.

September, 1937

TA·BAC

BELLS BEGIN RINGING

Bells begin ringing,
ephemeral among the trees
of afternoon outside my door.
Wheat pollen dulls
trembling gold into whitish
flatland thorns.
The circumference sways and lasts
as we leave our yearnings
for this day. Ranting
of lonely paths.
Clay and lime. Windows
of the house, shut
when I return at evening,
occasionally looking back.

ON MY DEATH

I'm weary of you, dark dominion
storm-tossed by flames.
I'll exhalt myself above horizons
and unfurl my flags in the desert
of this last charge on horseback.
Queen of these hours, now you come
all shining, armed.
Evening's useless desperation! Dawn
draws near with its sword,
and the mad ardor that inflames me
makes the stars grow dim.

"PERE QUART" (PEN NAME OF JOAN OLIVER)

(1899-   )

Born into a wealthy mercantile and banking family in the industrial town of Sabadell, Oliver has been an active leftist since the late 1920's. During the Republic, he was director of publications for the *Generalitat*, Catalonia's autonomous government. He also published regularly in a number of Catalan periodicals, including the *Sabadell Daily*, which he was editor-in-chief of from 1930 to 1934. With the end of the war, Oliver fled first to France and then to Chile. He returned to Catalonia in 1948 under a government amnesty, but for many years was denied a passport and could not legally leave Spain.

Oliver has published translations of Samuel Beckett, Anton Chekhov, and George Bernard Shaw, and has had a number of plays performed in the Catalan lands.

— García Lorca

Useless stars, useless bell!

Crippled time. Black night
windy, ashy, oily, porous.
Already in your felucca of invisible sails
— tightrope walker of swaying horizons —
you row, wander, digress
at the edge of an abyss
upholstered with fire and ice,
inferno of cold in closed eyes!

You, with your head in your hand, you were wandering
towards the summit, like a monstrous angel
haloed with grimy darkness
of patient days and nights made memorable
by love, leisure, or a dream.

You, with your head in your hand, you hid
behind the crimes of others' spotless hands,
generous with evil, with hideous caresses
of concave nails, red-hot, stuffed
with blackness ancient
as Eden's muddy slime.

You, with your head in your hand, you didn't know
Benito's shaken insolence
in complete uplifting, the chest puffed out
beneath the finely sculpted head,
the crown — rubies and emeralds —
of living bronze. A crown
for an empire of stuffed shirts.

You, with your head in your hand, you're a malignant shadow
or the frightening night's deceit.
The leftovers from this century's evildoing. The terrible
        memento
of a supreme gesture which might have abolished
shame itself.

Useless stars, useless bell,
far-off felucca with invisible sails.

Ding, dong!

PIG

I need a system for losing weight.
My skin's stretched taut, I get too winded.
I scarcely stir from home, I eat unspeakably:
obviously, I fatten like a hog
— such things happen—.
But, from now on:
no seconds, nothing with pumpkin in it
and a hundred pushups every morning.

They're already talking about St. Martin's Day.*

*A religious holiday on which pigs are slaughtered.

SONGS OF EXILE

One night when the moon was full
we crossed that hill,
slowly, not saying a word . . .
If the moon was full
so was our grief.

• •

My beloved is beside me
of dark skin and serious air
(like a Virgin Mary
found in the mountains).

• •

In Catalonia,
the day of my departure,
I left half my life slumbering;
The other half came with me
so as not to leave me lifeless.

• •

Today in French territory,
and perhaps still further tomorrow,
I won't die of longing
but longing will make me live.

• •

In my country of Vallès
three hills make a mountain range,
four pines a thick wood,
five towns too big a world.
"There's no place like **Vallès** "

• •

Let the pines ring the inlet,
the hermitage on the hill;
and on the beach a cloth to cover fish
beating like a wing.

      • •

A hope undone,
an infinite regret.
And a homeland so small
that I dream of it whole.

THE INTRUDER

"You enter my dream with a torch.
Servile shadows surround you.
You stand motionless, silent,
And voiceless, recall my crimes.

Speak if you can! Whip me
With all the names that have baptized my nights.
And if you can't, leave my dream.
Fear the dawn with its mastiffs.

Who are you? Serpent's eyes, rotten mouth,
Hellish cheeks and low forehead.
Queen perhaps of some desolate place
Or the bastard daughter of a glorious sin.

The shadows you command leap up.
Don't set them upon me.
Some are shy and obese,
Others bony with outstretched fingers.

The torch shines like an evil wish,
Lustful green, craven grey, frail white.
Blind shadows seek eyes and mirrors.
You, their mistress, smile silently.

It seems you advance! as if you're bending over!
The shadows hold their breath.
Who's that? What's that laughter?
You slide stiffly into my bed.

Get out of my night! Give me back the darkness!
Fear the dawn with its mastiffs!"

The fever is rising, the fever rises
In whirlwinds.

JANUARY PRAYER

(*Occidental rite*)

You are the Three, you are the Three
Wandering Salesmen.

The Blond,
champagne and capons from Prat.

The Black,
pearls and astrakhan overcoats.

The White,
chrome-covered cars and appliances.

Save Christianity
from Hell with a modest profit!

Oremus. . . .
(We'll say a patervoster
for those behind on their payments
and for their conversion
to the holy land of the dollar).

VACANCES PAGADES

He decidit d'anar-me'n per sempre.
Amén.

L'endemà tornaré
perquè sóc vell
i tinc els peus molt consentits,
amb inflors de poagre.

Però me'n tornaré demà passat,
rejovenit pel fàstic.
Per sempre més. Ame'n.

L'endemà passat l'altre tornaré,
colom de raça missatgera,
com ell estúpid,
no pas tan dreturer,
ni blanc tampoc.

Emmetzinat de mites,
amb les sàrries curulles de blasfèmies,
ossut i rebegut, i lleganyós,
príncep deposseït fins el seu somni,
job d'escaleta;
llenguatallat, sanat,
pastura de menjança.

Prendré el tren de vacances pagades.
Arrapat al topall.
La terra que va ser la nostre herència
fuig de mi.
És un doll entre cames
que em rebutja.
Herbei, pedram:
senyals d'amor dissolts en la vergonya.

Oh terra sense cel!

PAID VACATION

I've decided to go away forever.
Amen.

Tomorrow I'll come back
because I'm old
and have very sensitive feet
with swollen corns.

But I'll turn around the next day,
revived by disgust.
For ever more. Amen.

The day after that I'll come back,
like a carrier pigeon,
as stupid as he is,
not nearly as honest,
or as white either.

Poisoned by myths,
with saddle-bags full of curses,
skinny and rebuffed, sleepy-eyed,
a prince naked down to his dream,
Job of the pigsty;
tongueless, castrated,
pasturage for lice.

I'll take the train of paid vacations.
Holding onto the edge.
The land which was our heritage
flies from me.
It's a stream between my legs
that rejects me.
Grass, piles of stones;
love's signs dissolving in shame.

Oh land without a heaven!

Però mireu-me:
He retornat encara.
Tot sol, gairebé cec de tanta lepra.

Demà me'n vaig
— no us enganyo aquest cop —.
Sí, sí: me'n vaig de quatre grapes
com el rebesavi,
per la drecera dels contrabandistes
fins a la ratlla negra de la mort.

Salto llavors dins la tenebra encesa
on tot és estranger.
On viu, exiliat,
el Déu antic dels pares.

But look at me:
I've come back again.
All alone, almost blind from leprosy.

Tomorrow I'm leaving
— I'm not fooling this time —.
Yes, yes; I'm going on four paws
like a great-great-grandfather,
along smugglers' trails
right to death's black line.

Then I jump in the burning darkness
where everything is foreign.
Where the ancient God of our parents
lives in exile.

AGUSTÍ BARTRA

(1908-   )

Bartra came of age literarily during the Spanish Civil War, in which he served as a Republican soldier. He fled to France in 1939 and was interned in several concentration camps, one of which provides the setting for two poems included here. He remained in exile, mostly living in Mexico, until 1970, and the majority of his books were first published there.

In 1949, Bartra received a Guggenheim Fellowship that enabled him to compile an anthology of North American poetry in Catalan translation. Among his other translations are Castilian versions of William Blake and *Black Adam,* an anthology of Black French-language poets in Castilian translation. Bartra has also published novels, collections of short stories, and literary criticism.

During his period in exile, Bartra became one of the most internationally famous Catalan poets, yet he remained a half-forgotten figure in his own land. It is only in recent years, with his return to Barcelona and the publication of the first volume of his *Complete Poetic Works,* that he has begun to receive the recognition due him in Catalonia.

MANY

Many
> of those many who rose up
>> won't come back.

Many
> died blown to bits
>> and others, slowly, like tall
>> swaying trees,
>> lean
>> and crack from the axe-steel's
>> wounds.

Many died
> facing the stars,
>> others facing the mud.

They went into battle
> not to make their own lives more beautiful,
> but those of the unborn,

Many
> of the many who rose up
>> left mouths and sexes
>> that will call them.

They knew nothing
> of sciences, arts and letters;
> they regarded books
> as a luminous enigma
> shining on the other bank
> and though they didn't believe in the invention of God
> many of them signed their names with crosses.

They'll never again
                    slice bread at table,
                    or keep a bird in a cage,
                    or get tan at the beach,
                    or whistle from sidewalks.

No one will notice
                    their absence from the herded
                    crush of subways and streetcars,
                    or the clamor of playing fields,
                    or demonstrations of thousands and thousands.
                    But they'll push forward on the paths they opened
                    and in our collective awareness
                                        they'll be
                                        present
                                        and alive.

The same picks and shovels
                    that opened trenches
                    have opened their graves,
                    have dug the black earth,
                    the barren earth,
                    the virgin earth,
                    that was a dream of plowing,
                    of impossible fertilities.

And when they hid them
                    forever from the sunlight
                    the clouds filed by with syncopated
                    funeral march rhythms,
                    the ravens widened
                    their uneasy circles
                    and the wind brought weeping
                    from dried up fountains.

Many of those many who rose . . .

Lie
    wrapped in shrouds
    of their own lost blood
    awating new ardent days.
    Now they feel the roar of tractors,
    the rip of plowing,
    the golden wave of wheat stalks
    and the scythe's impatience.
    And by the power of unknown
    exploding seeds
    their clenched fists open
    into hands that help the fervent offering
    of igneous flowers to climb towards the light.

They haven't come back, nor will they
                          many of those many who rose up.

"PAVILLON TI". ALBA

S'ha romput el fil d'aigua del meu somni.
Per què aquesta claror de roses trèmules
dolçament embolcalla mon cor de pedra?
Per què vénen del record les falçs antigues
a segar camps, profunds d'anys i rialles?

Aviat cantarà la corneta:
                                   gall de tràgic metall!

Camp d'Agde, 1939

"PAVILION TI." DAWN

My dream's liquid thread has broken.
Why this brightness of trembling roses
sweetly enfolding my heart of stone?
Why do ancient scythes arise from memory
to mow the fields, deep in years and laughter?

Soon the bugle will sing:
                                   tragic metal cock!

Camp d'Agde, 1939

IN MANY PLACES OF THIS WORLD . . . .

In many places of this world there are great stretches of ripe wheat
with skies where songs sustain a sure and joyous flight.

In many places of this world the leaves are ardent lips
that kiss each cloud and speak to all the winds.

In many places of this world the day falls like an apple
— that the tree of night has ripened — of light and fragrance.

In many places of this world there are towers black with years and rain
with unmoving bells which hear each voice that rises.

In many places of this world love triumphs with its garlands,
and the seas calmly lift their waves' white joy.

In many places of this world the hours go by, weaving their dance
of tombs and cradles with a light untiring step.

In many places of this world, wheat, songs, leaves and bells,
love, cradles and tombs . . . Oh weary heart, what more do you ask?

Camp d'Agde, 1939

Great Comrade of the North, sweet giant of poppies and
        fog who sleeps, chaste and adamitic
like some young legend on the solar bank of your chants
        of horizons and flags:
give my your heart's
steel rose!

FALCON ABOVE A LAKE

Happiness of June:
you, house, boat and spirit.
And each leaf speaks
of the air's epic poem.

How strange my shadow
in flight towards dusk:
two wings, a crown,
an oar heavy across the muscle!

ALMOST A SONG

Light on seaweed
news of the day.

You still sleep.
I lift the wave
of one word,
then another. . .

I'm the sea,
you the wall.
With lips
of foam and air
I kiss the sail
of your spirit.

Sun on abandoned
boats. . .

SEVENTH ELEGY

AUTHOR'S NOTE: The corn-growing region extends from the village of Zoyatzingo to the slopes of the volcano Popocatepetl. Itzapapalotl was a goddess of the ancient Chichimec city of Cuayhtitlan, situated to the north of Lake Texcoco in the Valley of Mexico. Her name means "obsidian butterfly." She was a fantastic being bristling with stone knives. As a queen or mother goddess, she would appear to the desert tribes under a **mezquite** *(Prosopis juliflora), a tree resembling an acacia, or seated on top of "round cacti." According to a Nahuatl poem, she ate deer-hearts and turned into a doe.*

I

Unsleeping I walked, shrouded in wind,
crossing the sleeping city's outskirts
its slums
unvanquished in their dark flowing hair,
their flickering lamps and paper flowers
beneath an image,
and their countless feet of unshod earth. . .
Far away, a train whistled at the invisible moon.
Death sank his nails into black mud-brick walls.
Plaza. A rigid statue swung the fatherland
on a deserted fair's huge motionless Wheel
and two angels sought the Strongman's giant torso
in thirsty shadows
and the Puppet bent back his leap's
parabola.
Beethoven, in the ash tree, smiled upon his avalanches
and unleashed the hills of his might and tenderness.

I came with bluish dogs to the icy air,
to the plain where misty guerrilla women
ran, leaning forward, to meet the dawn.

II

Lying among lands of Toltec silences
I slept, I slept,
dreaming anew of five mythic suns . . .
Only the mountains had faces.
High wall of yearly harvests. Invisible,
Itzapapalotl walked on the other side.
She walked singing so her Nahuatl
would be sure to see the color of the corn;
she walked, tears falling on her naked breasts
assaulted by wolves, cracked by the dry season. . .

Standing by the wall, I waited awake
without time, in time through my pulse,
beneath the wind, full of the soul I had lived,
listening to yesterday's exodus in my blood,
the approaching deer of light. . .

And then at my feet, I saw the two Stars,
the sun, moon and tree,
and I rustled: "Touch my heart. . ."

I flung myself from fire to air like the snowflake of a trill,
entering the earth with a stalk of grain,
and lifting the water's thousand wings in the darkness,
I felled that statue which stank like a vulture.

SALVADOR ESPRIU

(1913-   )

Espriu is Catalonia's best-known contemporary poet. After a sickly childhood in which he was seriously ill for two years, he began publishing short stories and novels during the early 1930's. During that same period he studied ancient history and law at the Catalan Autonomous University, and was about to take a degree in classical languages when the Civil War broke out. He was then drafted into the army, where he served until 1939.

Espriu's first book of poems, *Sinera Cemetery*, appeared in 1946 in an underground edition. Like many of his stories, it focuses on the small village of Arenys de Mar, where the poet had spent much of his youth and which had been his parents' home town. Espriu's best-known play, *Esther's First Story*, was published two years later. It has been performed successfully both in Spain and abroad. In recent years Espriu has received the Montaigne Prize at Tübingen, the Spanish Critics' Prize, and the Grand Prize of Catalan Letters. He is currently Catalonia's prime candidate for the Nobel Prize.

Like Pere Quart, Espriu combines political consciousness with a kind of harsh lyricism. In Espriu, however, the imagery tends to be more brooding and death-conscious. Another distinctive element in his work is his use of the Old Testament. He has developed a series of symbolic parallels between Jews and Catalans, whom Espriu feels to be exiled from their collective identity even while they remain in their own land.

SUBURBAN SQUARE

This January evening
admiring other stars
I twisted my ankles.

Far-off hurdy-gurdies start to turn
dance tunes from a film with sound
to make house-maids swoon,
composed by priests
who enjoy the favor
of the most learned Catholic archbishop
of New York.

I see rascals with agile hands,
boxers — fly-weight class —
doings of love in the darkness,
taverns like pressure-cookers
with the breath of party-makers
ratafia-drinkers.

A woman, her fleshy
arms naked past the elbows,
shakes basins where olives swim
in khaki water.

I talk, chattering away
to myself in Catalan,
defunct language of funeral chants,
to give goose-bumps
to those with hearts like paper bags,
herds of fools in Terrassa,
grinding Cervantes' language
into pigeon droppings.

I am here,
like a one-eyed man, to shun the twinkling lights
of my frozen flat,
niche of memories,
painful disorders of thought.

I take strolls through the square
round solid citizens' houses,
killing time, while the Christian virtues
die in me.

When those behind the counters
return to their nests,
in great mystery
assemblies of old cats come to order
beneath captured bananas.

FROM *SINERA CEMETERY**

To Friede L. Martorell,
who also loved Sinera.

II

What a tiny land
encircles the cemetery!
This sea, Sinera,
hills of pines and vineyards,
dust in lanes. I love
nothing else, except a cloud's
drifting shadow.
The slow memory of days
that are gone forever.

III

Without name or symbol,
beside the cypresses, beneath
a bit of sandy dirt
hardened by rain.
Or let the wind scatter
ashes among boats
and the clear-cut furrows
and Sinera's light.
Brightness of April, of a land
that dies with me, as I watch
the years pass: a journey
through slow twilights.

*"Sinera" is an anagram for Arenys de Mar, a small
village on the Mediterranean.

VI

Spiders spun
kingly palaces,
rooms that trap
winter's footsteps.
Now Sinera's boats
no longer set forth,
because the water's pathways
have been destroyed.
For blind men's eyes
the sun cannot spread
holiday damasks
upon the ice.
Tiny bells no longer
ring down lanes.
I walk between rows
of cypresses.

IX

Flight of memories of rain
has sharpened the torture
of flowers dying
in the fragile harmonic passage
of afternoon and water.
How silent the sea is! Above it
triumph, fate, kingdom,
this prickly assault.
The cypresses gathered
the sky's wept brightness
into fleeting mirrors.

X

The arranger of rows
of cypresses and silence,
I'll confer the magic
scepter's serene authority
upon venerable hands.
Night wind, hymn, ancient
bronze against rain's
army, hard
solitude rediscovered.
Shepherd gods lead flocks
of docile clouds to the mountains.

XI

The light dies away, its
own offered mirror.
Flickering lights attract
    sluggish moths.

The night wind settled down
in the fields, in the cemetery.
When it awakens
    it will be a new day.

XIV

Crystal, memory,
the murmur of fountains, of clear
receding voices.
I watch the long afternoon,
with pauses of gold and dreaming.

XV

The bells' cold, slow ringing
spreads through the marsh.
Mist and crickets have conquered
all the afternoon's pathways.

XXIV

No eternalized waves
will be born in marble,
nor will flights of angels
arise from imagined empires.
For suddenly the evil season
is upon us. Memory's
voices lead me
through Sinera's empty rooms
to the watchman at dawn:
a cypress who knows the flames
of sea and cloud.

XXV

By the sea I had
a house, my dream.
By the sea.

High prow. Along
free pathways of water, the sleek
boat I commanded.

My eyes knew
all the calm and order
of this tiny land.

How should I need
to tell you the terror
of rain against windowpanes!
Now night's darkness
falls on my house.

Dark rocks
draw me toward shipwreck.
Captive of my song,
my effort wasted,
who can guide me to the dawn?

By the sea I had
a house, a slow dream.

XXVII

Dream, meaning, concrete
boats in the wind, the hard
word I still can
utter, between ancient boundaries
of vines and sea. I don't fight
life's effort,
for I don't know how. White walls
enclose me, peace lofty
and good beside the trees,
beneath dust and shadow.

DE TAN SENZILL, NO T'AGRADARÀ

Cansat de tants de versos que no fan companyia
—els admirables versos de savis excel·lents —,
i de mirar com passa l'emperador tot nu,
i del gran plany del vent, aquest vell adversari,
i de l'excés de mi, sense missatge,
ara us diré, amb paraules ben clares,
amb crit elemental, lluny d'artifici,
que vull només parar-me en el camí,
ja decantat amic de l'última injustícia,
i ajaçar-me per sempre, sense recança, mort,
damunt la bona terra.

SO SIMPLE YOU WON'T LIKE IT

Tired of so many verses which give no companionship
— the admirable verses of excellent sages —
and of watching the emperor pass in the nude,
and of the wind's vast lament, that old adversary,
and of too much me, with no message,
now I will tell you, in plain words,
with an elemental shriek, far from artifice,
that I want only to halt in the road,
already falling towards this last injustice,
and lie down forever, without regrets, dead,
upon the good earth.

L'aire resplendent
arrela en el plany.
Ales de la sang
drecen a claror.
De la llum a la fosca,
de la nit a la neu,
sofrença, camí,
paraules, destí,
per la terra, per l'aigua,
pel foc i pel vent.

Salvo el meu maligne
nombre en la unitat.
Enllà de contraris
veig identitat.
Sol, sense missatge,
deslliurat del pes
del temps, d'esperances,
dels morts,
dels records,
dic en el silenci
el nom del no-res.

The resplendent air
took root in the lament.
Wings of blood
lift towards brightness.
From light to dark
from night to snow,
suffering, pathway,
words, fate,
by land, by water,
by fire and by wind.

I salvage my hateful
number in unity.
Beyond contraries
I see identity.
Alone, without a message,
freed from the weight
of time, of hopes,
of deaths,
of memories,
I say in the silence
the name of the no-thing.

At times it is necessary and unavoidable
that a man die for a people,
but never does a whole people have to die
for one single man:
always remember this, Sepharad.*
Keep the bridges of dialogue safe
and seek to understand and respect
the diverse motives and tongues of your sons.
Let the rain fall slowly on the sown land
and the air pass, like an outstretched hand,
gentle and very benign, over the broad fields.
That Sepharad may live forever
in order and in peace, in work,
in difficult and deserved
liberty.

*A name usually associated with Spain, linking it to the Sephardic
Jews. In this poem it also serves as a euphemism.

TRIAL HYMN IN THE TEMPLE

Oh, how tired I am of my
craven old brutish land,
and how I'd like to get away from it
to the north,
where they say people are clean
and noble, learned, rich, free
wide-awake and happy.
Then, in the congregation, the brothers would say
disapprovingly: "Like a bird who leaves the nest
is that man who forsakes his place,"
while I, now far away, would laugh
at the law and ancient wisdom
of this, my arid village.
But I must never follow my dream
and I'll stay here till I die.
For I'm craven and brutish too.
And what's more I love, with a
desperate grief,
this my poor,
dirty, sad, unlucky homeland.

POEMA

JOAN BROSSA

(1919-   )

Brossa, at this moment, is one of the leading influences on young Catalan poets. He served in the so-called Catalan "baby bottle brigade" during the Civil War and then in 1939 was among the first Catalans drafted into Franco's army. In the late 1940's Brossa, the painter Antoni Tàpies, and other young artists would gather at a friend's house to read back issues of experimental art magazines. At that time Spain, following the lead of Nazi Germany, had outlawed "foreignizing art." In 1948, this same group began publishing an underground magazine, *Dice on Seven,* which represented the post-war reemergence of an avant-garde in Barcelona.

Since then, Brossa and Tàpies have continued to collaborate — most notably in the bitterly satirical *Novel,* a collection of official Spanish documents punctuated by Tàpies' sometimes brutal, sometimes mocking drawings. Brossa has also written extensively for the theater, and he helped stage some of the first "happenings."

SMALL APOTHEOSIS

The night
The day

We split the poem half
and half.

A mailman carrying the village correspondence
was surprised in the woods by
one of his neighbors who, brandishing a knife,
insisted that he gave him a certain letter, or that he let him have
the mailbag so he could look for it himself. The mailman
resisted as best he could and promised,
as was proper, that he'd bring the letter to his neighbor's house.
But the other refused, knocked the mailman
down, and started ransacking the mailbag when
a pair of policemen appeared on the scene
who, when they realized there was a fight going on, ran towards the men.
The neighbor fled and, chased by the policemen,
jumped over some rocks with so little
skill and luck that he broke his leg
fell on his back and hit his head on the ground.

Moments later a carriage pulled up.

THE KISS

It seems
that she breathes, at the very foot of the tree,
the obstinate grass. I pluck
a blade, trampled by many feet.
Here; take it as a memory
of this evening with me.

Poem
to be sculpted in lemon
wood.

And how did Daphnis
feel about Chloë's kiss?

PASTORAL

None, because the ones he didn't kill
flew away.

A shepherd fired into a tree
full of birds and killed some of them.
How many were left?

There still are flowers
and clumps of trees,
and a fountain to help
the trees and flowers grow.

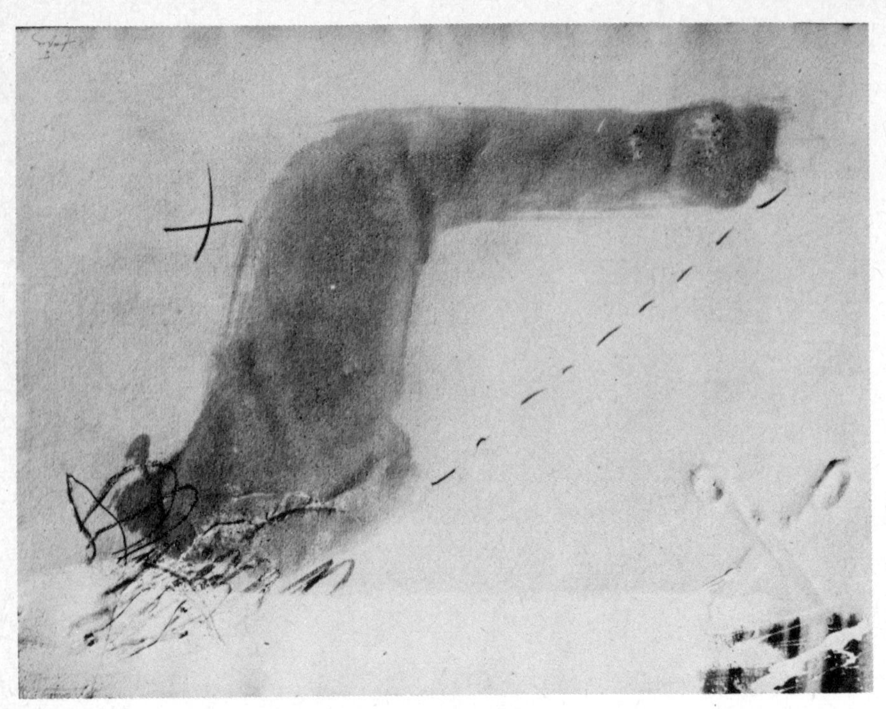

POEM WITH BLACK BACKGROUND

To David and Roser Mackay

To the right of the poem, a brown
sofa. In the middle of the poem,
Pierrot stretched out on the lines:
Harlequin crosses the poem, with
a black dove in his hand.
Colombine enters the poem
and from the sofa pulls dozens
of knitting needles.

She leaves.

TIME

This line is the present.

The line you've read is now past
— it fell behind after being read —.
The rest of the poem is the future,
which exists outside your
awareness.

The words
are here, whether you read them
or not. And nothing on earth
can change that.

LANGUAGE

I

Bread
There's a fountain beside the house
The wind roars

     ●

Two words
A description
An image

II

I'll call the moon and the sun
Gederme
and the men and the trees
Lungumul.

I stare at the fire . . .

I see myself walking past the end of the street,
all my money shot to hell.
She, I keep thinking, is with those clowns
who end up biting bullets
between the sea and the mountains. She's with those clowns
who end up biting bullets
between the sea and the mountains.

Terrible sea and impetuous! You
hold heaven's key
and lock up the waters underground.
Father of rain and storms,
you who are equal to the earth's own blood:
we adore you and invoke you.

A SPY WANDERS THROUGH THE STREETS OF WASHINGTON

A man wears an overcoat and grey boots.
A woman crosses, very pretty, in mourning.
A boy with glasses, near-sighted, explains with profuse
                  details
how it's he who's taken his place.
A man with a scar on his hand hurriedly leaves
                  a building
with a briefcase under his arm.
A bypasser complains that it's disgusting how they abuse the
populace in the street.
A boy passes with an old bent-over man.
A soldier, grim-faced, gets in a car which starts.
A woman walks into an optician's shop.
A man enters a phone booth.
Groups of young people pass.
A man with a mustache takes out his glasses.

DEFEAT

The rudder
gives direction to the ship.
The mountain is the ruin of a
country turned upside-down; the buildings
are underneath and their foundations
stick up.
      In the ruins
lies a buried people. If you listen
carefully you can hear
inside the mountain
a deep and
muffled voice
asking, always
asking.

You get up. Your silouette
hides the stars' reflexion
for a moment.

The prodigious silence of the sleeping
sea.

But
decisions must ripen
within people, not fall
from the sky.

VICENT ANDRÉS ESTELLÉS

(1924-   )

Vicent Andrés Estellés is usually considered the best Valencian poet since Ausiàs March. Despite the five hundred years separating them, there are some interesting parallels — in particular their rough, caustic language and obsessive treatment of sex and death. Estellés' work also reflects the special character of Valencia: more rural, more provincial, and more passionately "southern" than the Principality.

When Estellés brought out his first book in 1953, he was an isolated figure in a region that — though seventy-five percent of its three million inhabitants speak Catalan — had produced nothing of interest in that language for centuries. Since 1953 the Valencian situation has changed dramatically, partly through the influence of the folksinger Raimon and the essayist Joan Fuster, whose book *We the Valencians* provoked a radical shift of consciousness in his country. In the last few years, the number of Catalan language classes, theatrical presentations, and radio shows has doubled annually. It is in this context, and with the publication of his *Complete Works* between 1972 and 1977, that Estellés has come into his own, while the poetic resurgence he initiated has given rise to a whole school of gifted young Valencian writers.

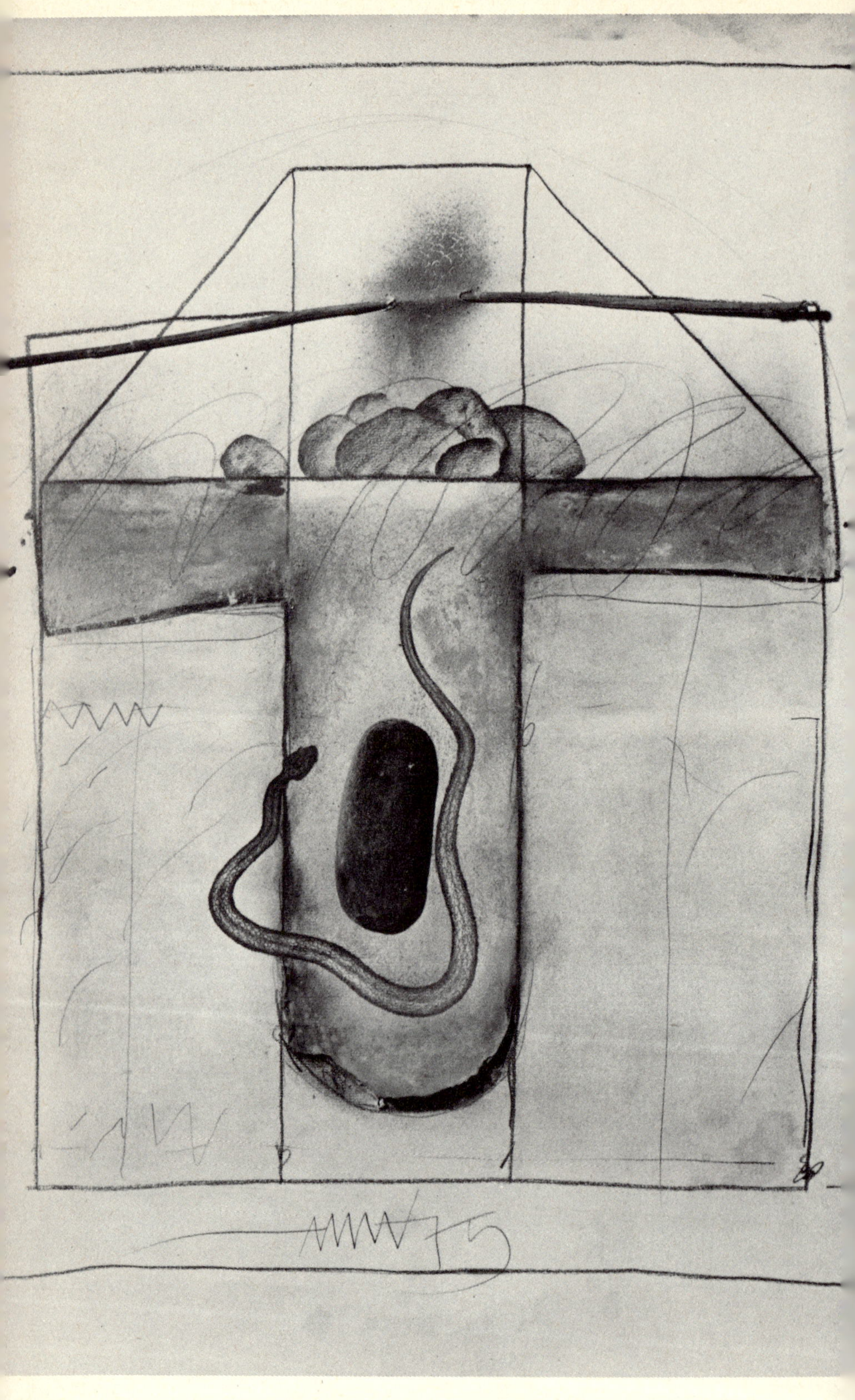

DECLARATION

The old boards
in the corridor groan.
The shadows pass
of angry poems
you decided not to write.

AUGURIES

You return, old grief,
familiar, intensely sweet,
and I can't complain.
Archaic beggars watch
over four live insomniac coals.

ENIGMA

It's raining against the windowpanes.
Nothing veils the rain.
An old sadness
unveils you —
objectified, they say.

FROM *HORATIANS*

For Eliseu Climent i Rosa

I

there's nothing i like as much
as garlanding roast peppers
with virgin olive oil.

then i sing happily, i talk to the oil, to the fruits of the earth.

i love roast peppers
— not too roasted, that ruins them —
but with the inside easy to get at
when you lift off the burnt skin.

i spread them on the plate in an exciting sequence
and garland them with oil and a pinch of salt
and i dunk lots of bread,
as the poor people do,
in the oil mixed with salt and flavored by the roast peppers.

then i pick up a bit of pepper
and a bit of bread between my thumb
and my index finger, i raise them avidly,
eucharistically,
i stare at them in the air.
sometimes i reach a point of ecstacy, of orgasm.

i close my eyes and gulp down the motherfucker.

i've never been afraid of death.
it's a fear i've never felt.
i've accepted in silence, without
writing elegies or necrologies,
the deaths of relatives
and friends. with the grave, mystery opened
its meanings. and i kept on, i went back to the streets.

an appearance of life.
i've never been afraid of death.
but now it bothers me.
i think about it sometimes, though not dramatically.
like hearing the wind in the buds, like someone who notices his
    eyes fill with tears while he's reading,
like someone who one day looks at his wife naked, worn out by
    childbirths.

what will remain of us all?

i'd trade everything for one fragment by sappho.

how will they see us?

maybe i'll be a roman clown.

si m'es permés,
evocaré dies de la infantesa.

furtava els fruits dels arbres.
me'ls menjava dins el dacsar,
fresc com un celler aleshores.

i sentia llunyana, pels carrers del meu poble,
la veu del meu pare que venia peix i cridava les veïnes.

era molt grat romandre allí.

m'envaïa una tristesa i una peresa.

de vegades venies tu
i t'agafava els pits, que m'agradaven més,
ens amuntegàvem i rodolàvem dins el solc.

m'oblidava de tot llavors, se'm feia de nit.

ja no oïa la veu del meu pare.
lladrava algun gos en alguna alqueria.

if it's permitted
i shall evoke the days of my childhood.

i stole the trees' bounty
and devoured it in the cornfield,
as cool as a wine cellar in those days.

and i heard far off, through the streets of my village,
my father's voice selling fish and calling the women.

it was real nice to hang around there.

a sadness and a laziness invaded me.

sometimes you'd come
and i'd take hold of your breasts — that was what I liked best,
we'd mount each other and roll around in the plowed field.

i forgot everything then, night fell on me.

i no longer heard my father's voice.
some dog kept barking in a farmhouse.

XXXVIII

i spent the afternoon and the evening drinking.

the wine inflamed desire, benign memories.

when i got into bed, i tried
to execute a coitus like the ones i'd remembered
but the wine, which inflamed my desire, also doused my potency.

six or seven times you cursed me.

finally i fell asleep while you tried to wake me up.

i can't imagine how you must have resolved it.

XLI

i lit a bonfire on the mountain top.
night came in like a ship.
slowly the fire went out.
now it's night on the mountain and
a fire still glows in the ashes.
i look at the firmament, i listen to
the night's small rustlings, memories
return. a dog barks
somewhere. i'm ignorant
of many things, the moon rises,
as in a certain elegy by ovid.
i evoke a few friends, fates
utterly diverse. our time:
  how will it be remembered?
  how will they judge it?

i slowly return from the mountain top to my house.

XLV

the sea painfully rocks the ships in the harbor;
their anatomy creaks.

light and smoke come from taverns
where people eat meat and drink wine.
a couple comes out with their arms around each other,
they share a long kiss
and go off down the street.
they'll lie down in the shadow of some vessel and do it.
shouts and out-of-tune singing come from the tavern.

tomorrow first thing in the morning we'll set out
a sailor tells me.

somewhere a pony whinnies.

LIV

my cousin came by today
with a record by raimon.

raimon sang
and the stone and the wind sang.

i squeezed isabel's hand.

when the record ended
my cousin was full of joy,
isabel and i were crying.

when will the gods or whoever put an end
to this situation.

i could rip out the walls.
isabel went in the kitchen

and brought me a glass of water.

puja la nit com un himne de safo.

he parlat molt amb el meu pare.
també, sovint, recorde aquells silencis
que creixien, normals, com un preny tranquil.
amb el meu pare he parlat de tot
allo' que hom parla amb un bon amic.
el meu pare em fou el millor amic,
sense deixar, però, mai d'ésser el
meu pare. no hi havia cap rigidesa
en la nostra relació diària, diversa.
em pense que això va assenyalar la
meua adolescencia. em divertien les
amables bestieses de l'ovidi, el pobre,
escandalitzant fins i tot els déus
més benevolents, però jo no ho hauria
sabut fer mai. sentia un darrer pudor.
el meu pare es preocupava perque' jo
estiguès bé de salut. potser la pàtria
o el cèsar o la cultura occidental un
dia podrien necessitar-me: havia, doncs
d'estar a punt per si això succeïa. he
tingut amigues i amants. mai no he
pensat que m'hauria pogut casar i ésser
un pacific espòs, un discret pare de
familia com en veig tants. mort el
meu pare, vaig continuar la vida que
feia. potser vaig escriure més bé o bé vaig
beure més o vaig buscar més els delits del
illit. ara pense que hauria pogut fer
discretament feliç una compatriota
dedicant-li un poema, fent-li un
fill, passejant amb ella ran de

la mar els blats les vinyes. estic
a punt d'estar trist. al cap al
tard em brillen les ninetes. sempre
espere el retorn del meu pare. o
potser el meu retorn a ell a casa
menjar unes olives trencades
  un pessic de formatge unes
    ametles un gotet de vi
    un poc de cada cosa
      res de res al
       remat en
        silenci
         ell
          i
          jo.

the night rises like one of sappho's hymns.

i've talked a lot with my father.
often i recall those silences too
that swelled naturally, like a tranquil pregnancy.
i've talked to him about all the things
a person talks about with a good friend.
my father was my best friend,
without ever ceasing, however, to be
my father. there was no rigidity
in our varied daily relationship.
i think this was shown by
my adolescence. ovid's pleasant
drivel amused me, the poor guy,
scandalizing even the kindest
gods, but i'd never have been able
to do it, i still felt ashamed.
my father worried about
my health. maybe the fatherland
or caesar or western civilization would need me
some day; i had to be
ready just in case. i've
had girlfriends and mistresses. i never
thought of getting married and becoming
a peaceful husband, a prudent paterfamilias
like so many men i see. when my father
died, i went on living like
before. maybe i wrote better or drank
more or went in more for the pleasures
of the bed. now i think i could have made
some compatriot happy by discreetly
dedicating a poem to her, giving her
a child, strolling with her beside

the sea, the wheat fields, the vineyards. i'm about
to get sad. at dusk
my eyes glisten. i always wait for
my father's return. or
maybe my return home to him
   to eat some broken olives
      a bit of cheese some
      almonds a glass of wine
         a little of each
         nothing at all
         polished off
          in silence
             he
             and
             i.

ILLICIT HOMAGE TO LLUIS MILÀ

To Francesc Brines
mas tendrán sentido
QUEVEDO

1

it's spring
joyous you outstripped nude
the water's trees

2

blackhaired myrtle
through the water returned a hawk from lisbon
oh moon moon moon

3

your body was gold
children's voices in the square
it was water

4

roughly he grabbed her hair
he dragged her along the floor towards the bed
the breeze rustled a curtain

5

her breasts were just emerging
she didn't dare look at them
like traffic lights

6

he looked at her one last time
the twilight was full of doves and grain
they'd beheaded her

7

the moonlight came in from the balcony
it sat down on the bed
and slowly took off its stockings

8

bull who runs loose through the field bull
green are the poplars
and there's a river nearby with singing washerwomen

9

don't go in the tavern
streetcars pass full of people
beneath an umbrella two lovers kiss on the mouth

10

intensely green trees trees oh trees
a fountain is heard among the leaves
under the bed your high heeled red shoes

11

you spilled onto the floor
there was a basket of oranges on the table
we loved to listen to mozart with the window open

12

the tango rose through her legs
it pinched her bellybutton
water streamed from her breasts

13

the goldfinch was singing oh mother how the goldfinch sang
the children whipped up the soap into lather
the bread fell in breadbaskets

14

the groom grabbed one of her breasts
he put it in his pocket
and left her forever on the corner of the avenue

15

up the wooden stairs up those stairs
the drunk was climbing carrying sailors' stories
the steps echoed like empty coffins

16

the logs came down the river
lovely was life lovely and very laudable the parson knew
taller than wheat the poppies burst forth

17

after committing the crime and washing himself
he went out to the movies
when the show ended they found him dead in his seat

18

sitting on the rug they passed the guitar
sweetly they strummed it they sang and rocked it
she unbuttoned her blouse for the five and gave her breast

19

alone in the house
she took off her shoes and socks and went barefoot
life's crazy sapling

20

she ironed in front of the window
falsely recalling an adolescence
he was a carpenter by trade

I see from back porches — domestic back porches
where family affairs are neatly displayed,
conjugal affairs, hygienic things,
and this with the clothesline's trembling syntax —,
I see from back porches, where starch is exalted
my pure Country, my only Country,
there, on the other bank, in the other part of the wind.
There are girls drying their long hair
and browning their backs and their thighs and their breasts.
The air's full of bottles with messages from the shipwrecked.

Now I'd like to write a nice poem
and talk about certain things you still can find that are nice
in my opinion, or according to the neighbor next door.
I want to be nice, today I want to say nice things.
I'd go through the whole house on my knees
looking for nice things, praying that today I'd be given
certain things that were really nice.
I've gotten out of the habit of nice things;
everyone knows what the things of this world are . . .
I've lost the habit, I don't know where I left them,
maybe at the café, maybe on a bench
by some promenade, it's possible, it's possible . . .
How can I know? But now it's night
and frankly it's no time to go out searching
for nice things, gentle things, nice things
precisely. The café's closed now,
the promenade is dark, you can find certain women
who want certain things, I'm tired, I'm not in the mood
to do anything, it's better to go to bed,
tomorrow'll be another day and by then I'll be over
this desire, this flaming mania
for nice things that's suddenly come over me.
That's suddenly come over me. I mean: that's come to me.

GABRIEL FERRATER

(1922-1972)

Ferrater received an eccentric education that included six months each year in the country and no formal schooling at all until he was ten. In 1938 his family fled to Southern France, where they remained until 1941. During the early 1950's, Ferrater studied mathematics at the University of Barcelona, while also publishing art criticism and essays. His first book of poems, however, did not appear until 1960. In the following decade he established himself as a leading voice in Barcelona, and was awarded the magazine *Serra d'Or's* Critics' Prize and the Gold Letter. His three books of poetry were collected shortly before his death in *The Women and the Days.* In 1972, for reasons that remain unclear, he committed suicide.

Ferrater's tone of voice – intimate and conversational – has been particularly influential in Catalonia. Its effects can be seen in such younger writers as Francesc Parcerisas and Marta Pessarrodona who, inspired partly by him and partly by North Americans, have introduced a greater personal directness into Catalan verse.

THE FURTIVE LIFE

Surely it will be like now. I'll be awake,
pacing up and down the foyer. Like a miner
leaving the shaft, it will rise
from the building's total silence, brusque,
the elevator's grind. I'll stop and listen
to the clang of metal doors, the steps
in the hallway, guessing the instant
when my doorbell-panic starts.
I'll know who they are. Then I'll let them in. All's lost,
let them enter. You have to tell them everything.

TWO GIRL FRIENDS

So much sun on ankles
and smooth, golden sea.
They hold hands,
saying nothing. Streets
of men, rancorous
for these girls know no man
of their kind.
Right now they're not going anywhere.
They return from the sun. They traverse
long afternoons, streets
of incomprehensible words.
They take away no memories.
They only want to know
that they're holding hands
and walk together, down a
foreign street.

A SMALL WAR

They brought anti-tank mines, useless
and heavy as an historic symbol,
wrapped in coverings soaked
with ancient smells, rosemary
and mule-sweat. And also German
machine-guns taken from fighter planes
and shells of English scrap metal.
In groups of two or three, widely separated
from each other, lowly and stubborn
as termites in a great felled stump,
the maquis bored through the Pyrenees.
It was one of the smallest wars
we've known. I came upon
only one corpse. That of a young
peasant girl from Aragon, who climbed in
an army truck, and also made
an easy symbol. She distracted
the driver and mechanic, and together the three of them
drove off a bridge. The girl
has a simple wound, nothing
interesting, but the doctors who did
the autopsy found a remarkable deformity
in her ankle, hereditary
in origin, drawn from far-off
roots in the racial tree.
And the pain of a moment, plus the pleasure
that brought it, lost importance
before that millenial defect,
deaf and established. Nothing individual.
It was a war, though a small one.
And fantastically enough, there was
nothing personal in it either, the nausea
that seized me, an instant's protracted examination
and with the sun's help, which fiercely
punished the covered nook and coarse
threshing-floor with its stubble of crosses and bones

which was that hamlet's cemetery,
when the stench of death seemed
the smell of some filthy sex. Meaning
I was young like all those
who go to war, and the flesh
frightens them, and they mangle and abuse it.
All emblematic, immemorial.

THREE LEMONS

Benign January. Beneath
so much green air, things
don't act surly today
nor is the place arid. look:
three lemons, placed
on the flagstone's roughness.
Because they're drenched in sunlight
and you can examine,
without doubt or haste,
the simple meter
that binds them together, do you think
they mean something?
Look, and already you've
grasped them.
     Captured heart,
from this moment on renounce,
be quiet. You won't make your own
this game of three lemons
on the flagstone's roughness.
Nor will you manage
to protest before you lose it.
No jolt of recollection
will abolish the calm
way of dying
that memories have.

WOMB

She's been here several hours now.
Parts of her body, not the most intimate
but parts of her body, are scattered
and divided among the four and twenty corners
of this room. And now I live
at the center of what I love.
Any movement I make, which pulls me
outside my fold, touches a stocking
or shoe or sweater or skirt:
the boundaries of my land.

IDLENESS

She sleeps. The time when men
are already awake, and little light
yet enters to wound them.
With little indeed we have enough. Only
the feeling of two things:
the earth turns, and women sleep.
Reconciled, we make our way
to the end of the world. We don't have
to do anything to help it.

MIQUEL MARTÍ I POL

(1929-   )

Martí i Pol is perhaps the most singular figure in contemporary Catalan literature. Born into a family of textile workers in Roda de Ter, a small mill town, he started work in a factory when he was fourteen. His wife still works in one, but Martí i Pol himself has been kept at home since 1970 by Parkinson's disease.

Martí i Pol grew up during a period when it was practically impossible for working class Catalans to become literate in their own language. Catalan was not taught in the schools, and people were fined for speaking it in the street. Nonetheless, he taught himself not only how to write it but how to write beautiful poetry in it. Much of his best work centers around the life of Roda de Ter, from which he draws a rich variety of human characters, images, and life stories.

In recent years, Martí i Pol's poetry has taken on a more somber and introspective tone. Confined to his house by illness, he has produced a body of work permeated by a sense of slow disintegration, self-enclosure, and his own daily battle to survive and keep writing.

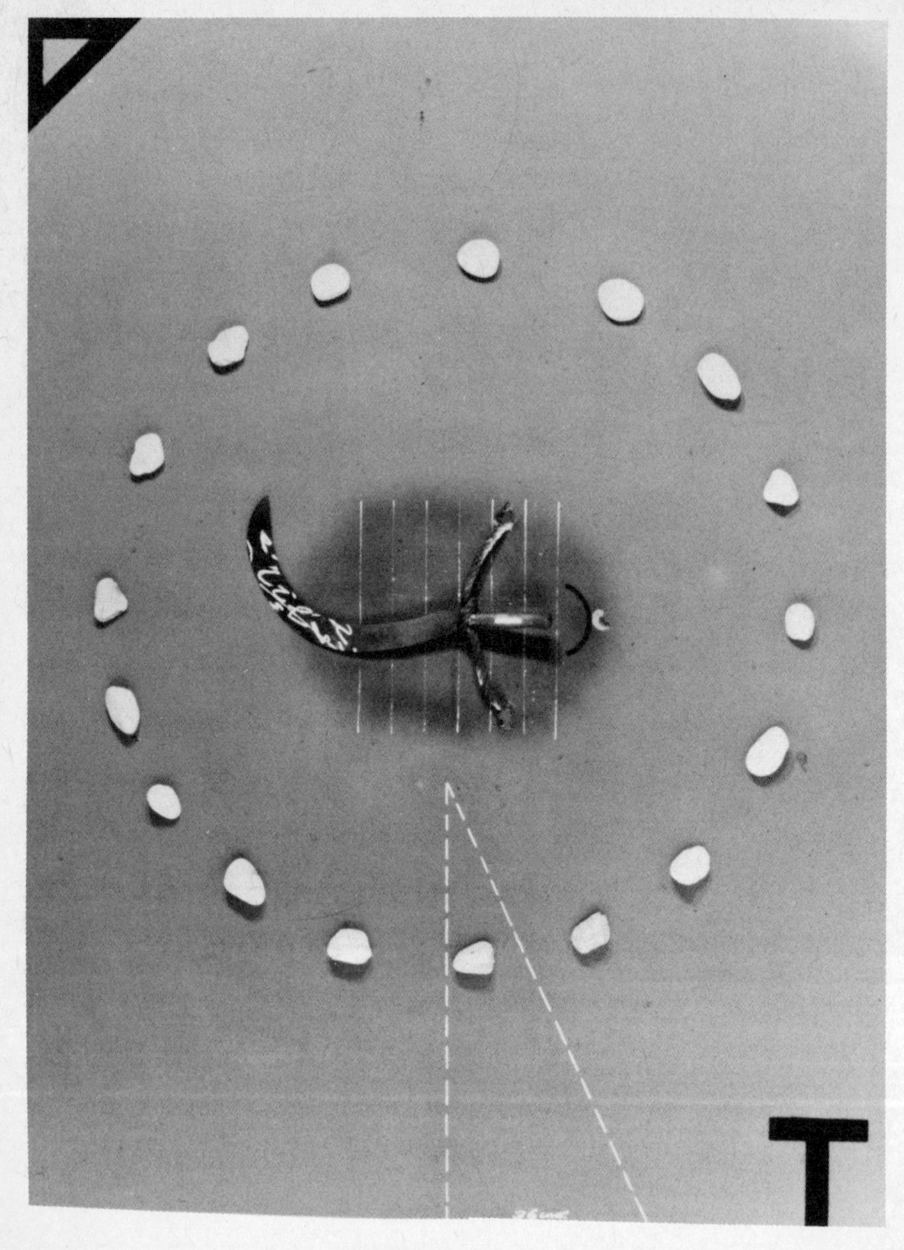

Neither longing nor distance
preserve you from the fire.
There are subtle precepts
behind each word
and great fear of the void
that attracts and frightens you.
In vain you walk
on the water's crest,
taste the bitter fruits
the foliage shelters
or climb the wind
up towards the highroads.
Sooner or later the night
will cut the moorings
of the ship you are
and launch you onto
clear paths of solitude
in the flame's dead center.
In the fire you'll uncover
whatever is inside you.

NOCTURN

A l'angle del carrer de París i l'avinguda de Roma,
al bar "l'Estrella", les vigílies de festa,
s'encén un rètol lluminós que anuncia
una beguda d'origen nord-americà.
El barri és nou i trist,
amb cases magres, desiguals, i un aire espès
amb tuf de cuina pobra.
Als carrers sense asfalt s'hi formen tolls
i la llum hi escasseja.
Molts diumenges al vespre,
l'amo del bar "l'Estrella" encén altra vegada
el rètol lluminós i s'embriaga.
La proclama, aggressiva, crema tota la nit.
Les dones que treballen
al primer torn i que es lleven de fosc
agraeixen el gest
amb un somriure de complicitat
carregat de tendresa.

NOCTURNE

On the corner of Paris Street and Rome Avenue,
at the "Estrella" bar, the night before holidays
a neon sign lights up advertising
a drink of North-American origin.
The neighborhood's new and sad,
with cheap, uneven houses, the air
thick with the stench of cheap cooking.
Puddles form on the unpaved streets
and the lighting is sparse.
Many Sunday evenings,
the boss of the "Estrella" lights
that neon sign again and gets drunk.
The aggressive proclamation burns all night.
The women who work
the first shift and get up in the dark
thank him for the gesture
with a smile of complicity
loaded with tenderness.

IN MEMORIAM

Since poems aren't always organized
around a subtle eddy
of conceits,
I can now say that today we buried
Soledad González
who for seventeen years had cleaned
the factory washrooms
and barely a year ago retired
because her legs would no longer hold her.

It won't help her any if I dedicate this poem to her.
And if I say she sang while she worked,
I'm just telling
facts of no importance.

Soledad González never
forgot her village in Extremadura,
and she said the acorns she'd shared
for years with the pigs she tended
were good to eat and nutritious.

Today it'd be easy to pile up miracles.
They threw Soledad
out of her village
when the war ended.

Everything lost is lost forever:
you, me, Soledad González.

SATURDAY

Every Saturday
the cool street air penetrates the houses
— the air's cooler and brighter on Saturdays —
and flushes from corners
the sadness
and obscure, routine effort
of the whole week.
Every Saturday
women open balconies and windows
and hang out bright colored clothes
as on procession days,
and with kerchiefs on their heads
like music hall Hungarians
they sing with lovely cries
while they polish the furniture
and expose their bedrooms' intimacy
to the neighbors.
If you go then through the streets
you'll think you're visiting an unknown village.
Women will smile at you amorously,
ready to love you with unsuspected tenderness.
This is Saturday's miracle,
absurd and slightly childish;
but everyone knows about it in the villages,
and every week homes are cleaned
and the cool street air
comes in through balconies and windows
and everything becomes beautiful again
by its virtue.

ELEANOR

Eleanor was
fourteen years and three hours old
when she started working.
These things remain
stamped in your blood forever.
She still wore braids
and said "Yes sir" and "Good afternoon."
People loved her,
Eleanor, so gentle,
and she sang as she
hurried her broom.
But the factory years
fade in the windows'
opaque greyness,
and after a bit Eleanor didn't know
where her urge to cry came from
and that uncontrollable
feeling of loneliness.
The women said she
was just growing up and those ills
were cured by getting married and having children.
Eleanor, in accord with the women's
wise prediction
grew up, got married, and had children.
The oldest, who was a girl,
just three hours
after her fourteenth birthday
started working.
She still wore braids
and said "Yes sir" and "Good afternoon."

NOTICE

All ground floor
and first floor workers
will enter and leave the factory
through the main door.
The main door
is the exit and entrance door
for all workers.
All other doors
may be used
at the worker's discretion
but not
to enter or leave the factory
at the beginning
and end of the shift.
Starting next Monday
each worker
as he enters
will collect his card
from the box that matches his section.
He will then punch in on the time-clock
following the abundant instructions he has received
and will return the card to its place.
The cards and the time-clock
are at the bottom of the staircase
inside the main door.

SUMMER

Now's the time to love on pathways
by the side of the river, where the grass is soft and welcoming
and in the shade of old trees
by half-lost fountains
where the woods are most secret.

Now's the time to sit by the street
and talk about soccer and women
after supper
in groups by the narrow curb,
watching the girls
as they cross the street towards us
and pass by and disappear
a little skittish.

Now's the time of carpenters and plasterers
time to sing while working
in the bright sun
forgetting the scaffold's risk
forgetting the effort
and the monotony of work and life.

Now's the time to take the girls for walks
and the wife, wearing white gloves
to hide the ravages of bleach,
on Sunday afternoons
along the road flanked with plane trees
saying hello to everyone
with great nods of the head,
envying the wives of those you pass.

Now is the time of women sewing
in the half-shadows of entrances
often dozing above their work,
and the time of men napping
in the house's darkest corner

on sunny afternoons
when the streets are dense with silence
and the heat is ruthless.

Now it's summer:
solid summer, a little absurd
but intensely beautiful
coming suddenly
any night around the start of June
and leaving, also suddenly,
any night at September's end.

WORDS

Words don't always mean the same thing.

The distance from one place to another is variable.

You and I can't sit in the same chair.
And now, on their knees,
let everyone beg forgiveness.

Only order guarantees justice.

Morality is the safeguard of freedom.

You and I — hadn't you heard? —
can't sit in the same chair.

FIRST INTERLUDE

With a dirty shoe, thrown from a
prudent distance, you can safely
shatter the mirror on the wardrobe.

Don't bother picking up the pieces.
Leave the room. Close
the door, lock it, and throw
the key in the river.

If when you're outside you hear a cock crow,
don't be afraid, he just wants company.

I know little about myself. Maybe
that's why I could now
sell my body, which barely keeps going.
I still don't dare to hack myself to bits.

A dog barks outside
and the wind slips through doors.
It'll make the reeds whistle,
if that clearing by the water is still the same.

There's no present;
all paths are memories or questions.

METAMORPHOSIS – II

The man I am looks at me with rainy eyes.
The man I am inhabits me strangely.
Hard to shake, he's ivy that grows
on my skin, hard and black.

*   *   *

Along my own flank I climb down into the well
carrying myself piggyback as best I can,
wiping telltale signs and traces
from the walls. Then I use my walking stick
as a lever and raise the water up
and it all spills at the well-mouth. Once again it is I
who make the afternoon fertile.

*   *   *

The man I am wears a beard of centuries,
so soaked with twilight and tides
that no bird will make his nest there. He claws
my flesh open so the wind can enter
to heal my wounds with living salt.

ALGAE IN MY EYES

Let's suppose there are still innocent doves
and people cured only by teas
and four or five pure damsels
and a vessel that never sets sail from port
because of fear of tides. And let's say
three lightning rods make a futurist forest,
and a sea of roof-tiles a deep ocean,
and two sparrows a world full of hope.
Let's even say that if I close my eyes
I see a naked transparent girl,
and that behind her, there where the shadow
seems densest, deepest,
if I shut my eyes hard, bouquets
of flowers suddenly explode, and she laughs.

FRANCESC PARCERISAS

(1944-   )

Percerisas is a highly prolific poet who has brought out six books in the last nine years. He has lived in the United States, Mexico, and England, where he taught at the University of Bristol. He now makes his home in Iviza, where he and some friends share a large house they built with the help of a local mason. Parcerisas has collaborated extensively with Arranz-Bravo and Bartolozzi, two young Catalan artists who have exhibited in such foreign capitals as Stockholm and New York.

In many ways, Parcerisas and his generation represent the re-emergence of Catalan culture from the dark tunnel of the postwar era. In his work, one can feel a new gaiety and self-confidence, an easy familiarity with international culture, and an increased freedom in talking directly about his inner and sexual life.

Joseph had died of cancer two years before.
No one kept up the struggle, no one started picking up bundles again
    at the printer's shop,
passwords weren't given out, nor was that weak, slightly fanatical
    comrade loved in secret.

"Times had changed. Political struggle,"
he said, "had become something totally different."
I kept quiet.

Afterwards, it turned out that the lawyers found the right legal
tactics for the trial. It seemed like one of the organization's finest
jobs. But at the last minute circumstances changed, it happened one
night, at an especially important meeting. . .
"I already knew about the rest."

Meanwhile the girl at the bar brought another bottle,
the air was chilly and the bar filled up quicker.
I was grateful to him for not mentioning my now-declining fame.
"I know. Just one word and everything starts up again."

Through the foggy windows you could see the cars' headlights
shining as they turned onto the main street, night was falling.
"Tomorrow I'll go down to the office and legalize my situation," I
    told him.

                    The girl at the bar had started singing
a popular song.

MICE

We've got a fire and some friends.
We've drunk a little too much
and naturally we're more lucid.
Now we can do something good,
it doesn't matter what, something great.

We can do something good
and since we're lucid and we know it
we talk about it all night long
and the night never ends.
By dawn we've missed our chance
and we decide to go swimming.

Drowsy and laughing, the cook
comes to show us a mouse
caught during the night
in a trap she'd set for it.

MOVIE HOUSE: THE MALACHITE KIOSK

Sometimes it's the crystal air at the beach,
the pearly drinks that surprise the sensual amber
of your lips, opened by the body's mystery
love of palmtrees and lilacs on the coast
a white telephone by the suicidal bath
resigned emotional adventure
on the express train
scorned nocturnal romantic invitation absence
mint divans and old Frank Sinatra sides
or they'll be the same staircases, all with balconies
where the twinkling city lights put us to sleep
the bright splendor of curtains our union
love's morning recognized early morning love.

With your conscience soothed you leave the theater
dreaming, unhappy, of another country, traps.

PASTORAL

La penetro a mig matí, la feina interrompuda,
interrompuda la domesticitat de totes feines:
tot és desig d'amor i or i alenar robant-nos el mot farfallós.
    (que no ens sentissin els infants, amor,
    juguen al pati, ara, ells, corren, saben
    que som a la cambra, amagar-se, ells, amagats,
    amor, corren, en la urgència del joc, ells renunciant,
    ells, amor, al nostre amor ombriu)
¿Es que la mutació còsmica ens bressa,
bressa el temps i del temps els subterfugis?
¿Són tot cingles, austeritat i cendres?
Sentir el dintre fora, en tu,
i el fora dintre meu, profund.
All sublunary creatures do Her
(Venus) living homage, in their kind.
    (juguen els infants a l'espai exterior,
    amor, el nostre amor, els crits,
    fruites que són, ells, dolçor de jocs,
    ara els infants juguen, ara, ells,
    fruites són, contacte animal,
    el nostre espai: interior)
Esclata la fanfàrria: oh, els crits,
la neu, la joia, els crits anunciant-les,
els cossos oferts, rendits parracs d'amor,
les nostres mans prement-se, joveníssims amants,
tot és present i nit d'ocells.
    (que juguin i escampin meravelles,
    corren els infants, ara, ells,
    el nostre amor, meravelles, obert convit,
    ara jugant, amor, sense secrets,
    escampant amor, ells, a mig matí,
    ara, el nostre amor penetren)

PASTORAL

I enter her at midmorning, my work interrupted,
interrupted the domesticity of all our work.
All's desire for love and gold and to breathe stealing
          the garbled word from us.
    (don't let the children hear us, love,
     they're playing in the courtyard, now, they, run, they know
     we're in the bedroom, to hide, they, hidden,
     love, run, in urgent games, they, renouncing,
     they, love, our shadowy love)
Does cosmic mutation rock us,
rocking time and time's subterfuges?
Is everything cliffs, austerity and ashes?
To feel the inside outside, in you
and the outside deep within me.
All sublunary creatures do Her
(Venus) living homage, in their kind.
    (the children play in the space outside,
    love, our love, the cries,
    fruits they are, they, sweetness of games,
    now the children play, now, they,
    fruits they are, animal contact,
    our space: inner)
The fanfare bursts forth: oh, the cries,
the snow, the joy, the cries announcing them,
the offered bodies, yielded rags of love,
our hands gripped tight, the youngest of lovers,
all is present and night of birds.
    (let them play and scatter miracles
    the children run, now, they,
    our love, miracles, open invitation,
    now playing, love, without secrets,
    scattering love, they, at midmorning,
    now, they penetrate our love)

A NARROW ROOM, TRIANGULAR IN SHAPE

Like that famous table of contents I spoke of, your body's
a penetrating word, bearing fruit in me like sperm's
eternal right to rain new life. Lips of salt
and moss of breasts are the discharge of dreams lived
in fear, and in silent words of very narrow whiteness.
A chisel of moons dividing the night, and embrace of hopes
that the flesh cannot bear, are the seed of sunny lands
and sea-borne promises, of differences praising each man's
tragic heritage. Night's shrunken light harbors
easy sweat, a tongue of fire split into bodies.

LEAPING DOLPHINS

Dolphins leaping at prows in Tagomago's*
waters, deep, scatter their loins'
salt spray, seeking the atmosphere's warmth.
Whirlwind of blues and oxygen of spume
piercing the early blue, he rises green,
calling his comrades to their mad race
against the boat's horsepower. Dolphins
that leap fleeing the alien keel
in their domains, are the example
I've sought in the sea, to tell you
of men's rare happiness.

*A small island northeast of Iviza.

WITH THE HOUSE LOCKED

They tell me the cypresses, ripped and black
with smoke, have been cut down to heat
the blind sogginess of prison guards. I also remember
the locked house, the benches and chairs
shiny with clever discourse, it was the golden age
and the air full of hopeful predictions.
Like some old story in the dead of winter: "Time
was time, disturbing words kept falling and
spontaneous generation gave us some excellent
pen-strokes. . ." Like a biblical prophecy.
Now flies hover near the corpse, decomposing
in the middle of our widest street, now inner
doors declare you *doctor honoris causa*.

MARTA PESSARRODONA

(1941-   )

Like Parcerisas and virtually all of their generation, Marta Pessarrodona was educated in Castilian and had to teach herself to write Catalan. She began publishing in 1965, and her most recent book, *Private Life*, has almost sold out its original edition of 1200 copies — a case not unusual among young Catalan poets, and which puts her at least on a par with her average North American contemporary.

Pessarrodona met Gabriel Ferrater in 1968, and up until his death in 1972 their relationship was an intense and inspiring one. She now writes for the newspapers *Daily World*, *The Barcelona Daily*, and *Today*, as well as for the feminist magazine *Vindication*. One of her plays was recently produced on Spanish television. Despite their considerable differences, Pessarrodona's work resembles that of Parcerisas in its receptiveness to English and North American influences and its subjective immediacy.

THE A.B.C. OF THINGS

Long apprenticeship,
that of cynicism.

Any faith
will repay you in coldness,
and the winter goes on,
it lasts too long.

You'll live as you must
to see
contraries meet.

And if you're a poet
you'll get involved
in little things,

You'll shout about small
injustices and all the political parties
will disown you.

Your friends will be your censors
and yourself,
emboldened by seeing,
for the first time,
that the earth turns,
and that nothing
nothing stops it.

LANDSCAPE WITH OBESE FIGURE

Lost, that written faith,
slaves of the casual lump of earth,
the obese priests
of cult and ritual
of useful friendships,
hand down the laws
of obedience or death:
this familiar ending:
a gaping hole, silence.

And it's useless to hide,
to avoid the daily papers,
to dine with very few people,
to write with disappearing ink,
to recite verses in a low voice.
They've given the final
sentence: to banish us
from this their putrid, telephonic,
enterprising kingdom.

THE CRUELTY OF THE MONTHS

I know I can allow myself, let us say,
certain luxuries: it was a room
at almost four P.M.
From the shelter of afterwards, I make
a promise never to forget it.
I've spent many hours going over
that room in my head.
The clock was living: nothing else.
Color of gold I detest: really
give me the silver, if possible
old and English and stolen.
Strange and frozen spring.
I've lived through such hours of cold
hating, passionate, Matthew Arnold.
(I didn't even see the rocks
and the Nordic light was too clear)
Comprehensible things
and sensible people
don't interest me now.
No one can help me.
Marie, Marie, hold on tight!
And now you know it all and more:
everything began and ended
— I really don't know what —
in April, in that room.

NIT TRISTA DE SANT JOAN

No vam saltar ni l'última foguera.
Nit sense sorolls ni xiuxiueig de brases.
Nit de somnífer, letífer remor.

   (Quant de temps ha calgut
per saber cobejar el corb
—aquest literari animalot
de color d'ala de mosca?)

   Nit per no viure-la:
dolor adéu, adéu amor.
Ho haviem cremat ja tot.

SAD ST. JOHN'S EVE

We didn't jump even the last bonfire.
Night without sounds, without crackling coals.
Night of drowsy, poisonous rustling.

   (How long did it take
the raven to learn greed
— that literary beast
fly wing color?)

   Night not to be lived through;
grief farewell, farewell love.
We'd already burned it all.

RAMON PINYOL

(1950-   )

Pinyol is a leading figure among Catalonia's youngest group of poets. His cultivation of the sonnet is part of a widespread attempt to reach back into the Catalan literary past, towards figures like Ausiàs March, Jaume Roig, and Joan Roiç de Corella, linking them to modern attitudes at the same time.

Pinyol has published four books of poetry. He is also the owner and editor-in-chief of Mallet Books, a publishing house dedicated to bringing out young poets, foreign literature in translation, and modern classics like Brossa's and Tàpies' *Novel* or Martí i Pol's complete works. For the past year, he has been in charge of a television program devoted to Catalan culture.

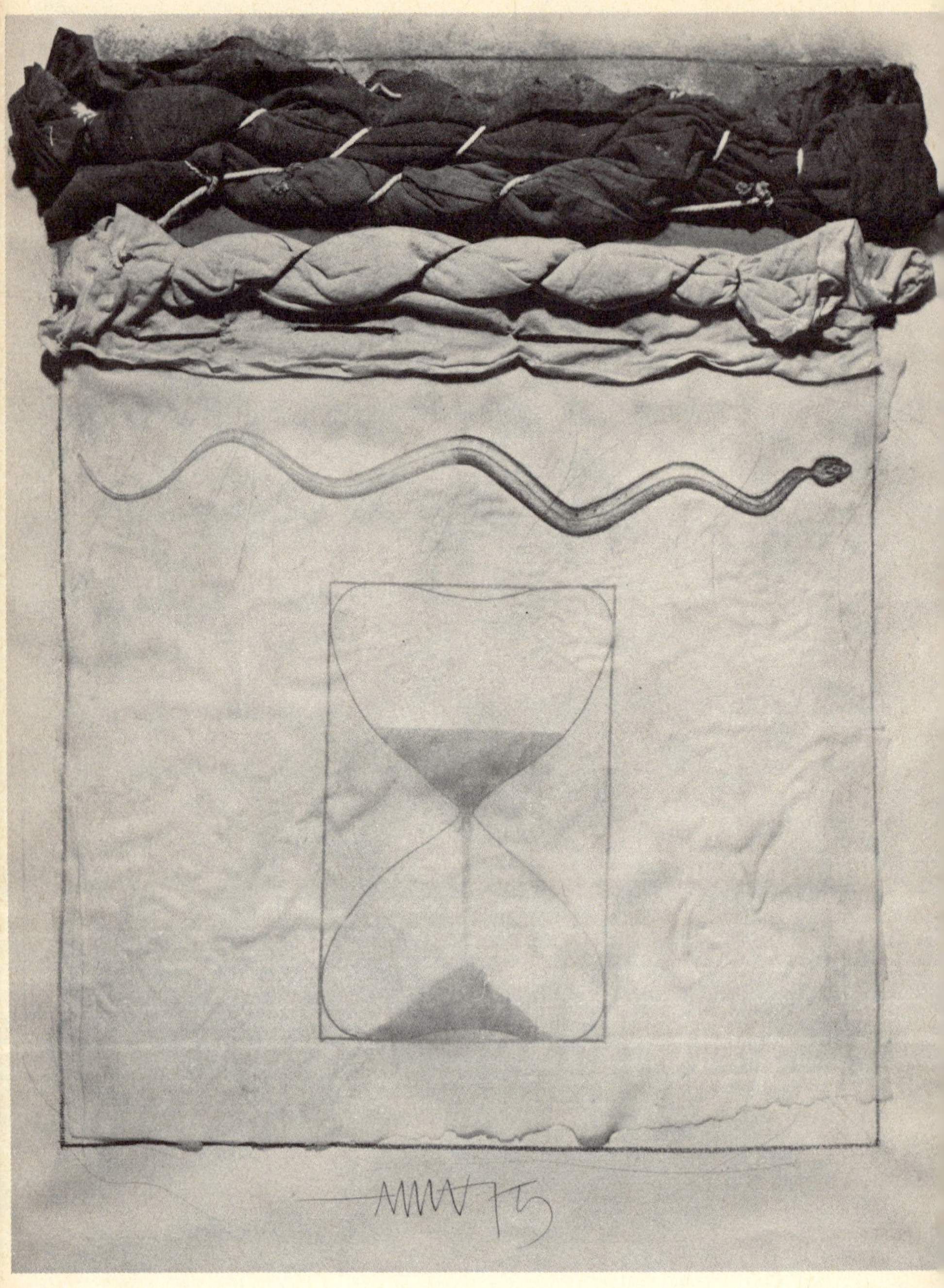

SENSELESS ONES

Senseless ones,   workers lame and ignorant,
by God, we'll make   the revolution.
We'll attack   both warders and jail,
armed with cries   with arrows of chant.

The assaulters   of dreams fall wounded,
the true, the lovely   what is just in the ripeness
of nation and years.   Only deaf men talk. We don't hear
the redeemer's song.   Enough of beggars.

What we take   is thanks to no one.
Rebel repose.   Yeast in a time of ovens.
Raise your fists!   Let us make our bread!

Thieves by law   machines of hunger
we kill!   Let the horn sound loud:
bosses to work,   no more lords: our cry!

EL NUS DE L'HORA

Et trobaré   on el pou no mor mai,
on l'aigua neix   i és sempre clara i fonda.
La meva set   no estroncarà la deu,
que la mercè   brolla sempre i per sempre.
Sempre, tostemps,   etern el nus de l'hora.
Jo me'n desfaig,   que és meu el temps d'amor,
la nit és jorn,   la mort esdevé jove.
Puix que tresbals   vol dir bots vells, bots nous,
no hi val pedaç: ho diu el de tot pare.
I jo, antic,   aprenc la lliço' vella,
de nou al tomb,   gosat i sense espera.
Amara amor!   Perquè estimem l'hora
de l'U i el Tot,   l'aigua, la rel, el pou,
un pas de mar,   la barca damunt l'ona.

THE HOUR'S KNOT

I will find you   where wells never die
where water is born   and is always clear and deep.
My thirst   will not dry the fountain
that grace feeds   forever and ever.
Always, forever,   eternal the hour's knot.
I undo it   love's time is mine,
night is day   and death becomes young.
Since good wine   needs skins old and new,
no use patching the old   god himself will tell you.
And ancient,   I learn the old lesson,
once again at the front   daring and restless.
Love brims over!   For we love that hour
of the One and the All   the water, the stem, the well,
a trip on high seas   the boat on the waves.

YOUR SERVANT

It pounds in my head: cunts, fucking pigs!
Shameless. My chant — your lord,
your servant, of all nations —
wants me this way, obsessed by this bulging!

Can you plane so many knots, my son?
How can I get through such knots and swamps?
Give up? I don't say no, but
I can't lie down, or hide in my caste.

These bastards fling us their nets!
And in green and grey uniforms scatter barbs
everywhere, evil weeds from this

land of pus, pus-filled faces,
silver-stuffed chests, bulging with medals.
They spit sterile fire through the fields!

"MIQUEL DESCLOT"(PEN NAME OF MIQUEL MUÑOZ)

(1952-   )

Desclot is the youngest poet in this anthology. He has published two volumes of verse and several children's books. Like Pinyol, he is active in a young publishing house (Ausiàs March Editions) dedicated mainly to bringing out new poets.

Both Pinyol and Desclot are equally at home with traditional and open forms. In this sense, they represent the double thrust of the newest generation of Catalan poets: to reinvestigate their literary past, while at the same time continuing to develop Catalan's rich experimental tradition.

**SHE, THE IMMORTAL FAIRY, APPEARED TO ME
SUDDENLY AND WITH HER HARPOON OF LIONBONE
PIERCED MY DROWSY PUPILS**

I'd board the train
and be off
to the North, swiftly
seeking a star
that might fill
this empty glass.
I'd take another
and slide
forever towards the South,
inscribing palmtrees
on the parched earth's
brown behind.
And yet another
to be able to flee
towards the light of the East
and enter the womb
of summer days
of winter and fall. . .
I'd push on to the end
and doze
along Western trails,
till I reached the tomb
of sunny days
and moonlit nights.
All these trains of mine
would derail
in a chaos
of total fantasy.
The immortal fairies
would console me.

**IN A MIGHTY WAVE OF STICKS AND BOULDERS SHE
LOST HER SCALES, ONE THURSDAY WHEN THE SUN WAS
VERY HIGH. SHE IMPROVISED SOME OTHERS WITH A
SWORD AND TWO TILES, AS THE SUN WAS ALREADY
SETTING.**

Those upright black leather lightning-bolts
undid your rye-braids
beneath the sun's insulting truth.
Unwinged, your gazelle-heels.
a horse's boot made you bend
your knees, pale with terror.
You fell like a wounded partridge.
All the dogs, greyhounds and setters,
attacked your unmoving body:
they tore the fineness from your breast
—whiter now than a frozen moon —
they bent the serenity in your bones
— which moments before had made you brave —
and dimmed forever your blackbird-eyes,
they bruised your womb of grain.
When the hunters all arrived
they bound your hands and feet with straps
to dangle you like some prey.
When they saw the eagle's shadow in the sun
they said a wolf had killed you. . .
On your blanket of earth
the usurer's-fingers of cypresses clutch
the sun's last three coins.

SELECTED BIBLIOGRAPHY

Works available in English:

Bartra, Agustí. *Marsius and Adila.* tr. Elinor Randall. Mexico City: El Corno Emplumado, 1962.
Colomer, Jordi. *Diccionari anglès-català.* Barcelona: Pòrtic, 1973.
Espriu, Salvador. *Lord of the Shadow.* tr. Kenneth Lyons. Oxford: Dolphin Book Co., 1975.
Gili, Joan. *Catalan Grammar.* Oxford: Dolphin Book Co., 1976.
Riba, Carles. *Poems.* tr. Joan Gili. Oxford: Dolphin Book Co., 1970.
Rosenthal, David H., tr. "Four Modern Catalan Poets," *New Directions 31.* New York: New Directions, 1975.
Terry, Arthur. *Catalan Literature.* London: Ernest Benn Ltd., 1972.
————————————, tr. *A Small War and Other Poems.* Belfast: Festival Publications, 1967.
Triadú, Joan, ed. *An Anthology of Catalan Lyric Poetry.* Oxford: Dolphin Book Co., 1953 (texts in Catalan, introduction in English).
Yates, Alan. *Catalan.* London: Teach Yourself Books, 1975.

The poems translated here are available in the following collections:
Bartra, Agustí. *Obra poètica completa.* Barcelona: Edicions 62, 1971.
Brossa, Joan. *Poemes de seny i cabell.* Barcelona: Ariel, 1977.
Cartwright, Stephen, ed. *Poesia catalana de la guerra d'Espanya i de la resistència.* Paris: Edicions Catalanes de Paris, 1969.
Castellet, Josep M. and Joaquim Molas, eds. *Poesia catalana del segle XX.* Barcelona: Edicions 62, 1963.
Desclot, Miquel. *Ira és trista passió.* Barcelona: Amadeu Oller, 1971 (Edition of 500 copies, not on sale publicly).
Espriu, Salvador. *Obres completes I: poesia.* Barcelona: Edicions 62, 1968.
Estellés, Vicent Andrés. *Obra completa.* 3 vols. Valencia: Tres i Quatre, 1972-77.
Ferrater, Gabriel. *Les dones i els dies.* Barcelona: Edicions 62, 1968.
Foix, J.V. *Obres completes I: poesia.* Barcelona: Edicions 62, 1974.
Martí i Pol, Miquel. *Obra poètica.* 3 vols. Barcelona: Llibres del Mall, 1975-77.
Parcerisas, Francesc. *Discurs sobre les matèries terrestres.* Barcelona: Edicions 62, 1972.
__________. *Homes que es banyen.* Barcelona: Aymà, 1970.
__________. *Latituds dels cavalls.* Barcelona: Lumen, 1974.
Pessarrodona, Marta. *Vida privada.* Barcelona: Lumen, 1972.
Pinyol, Ramon. *Aigües d'enlloc.* Barcelona: Edicions 62, 1973.
__________. *Remor de rems.* Barcelona: Amadeu Oller, 1972 (Edition of 500 copies, not on sale publicly).
Quart, Pere. *Obra.* Barcelona: Fontanella, 1963.
Salvat-Papasseit, Joan. *Poesies.* Barcelona: Ariel, 1962.

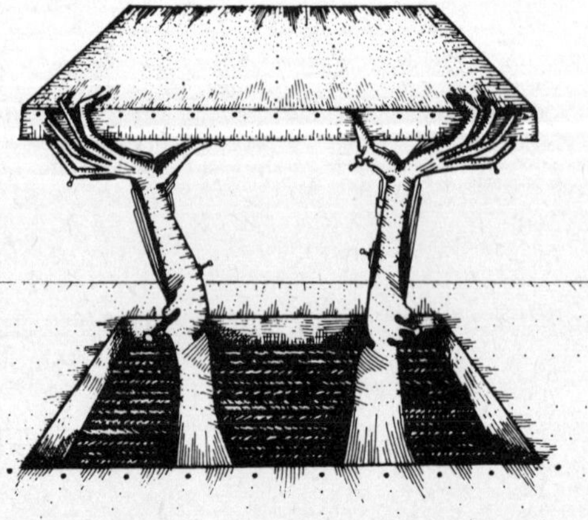